DEBBIE BROWN'S
Saucy Cakes

DEBBIE BROWN'S
Saucy Cakes

HAMLYN

To Paul, for all the giggles

First published in Great Britain 1993
by Hamlyn an imprint of Reed Consumer Books Limited
Michelin House, 81 Fulham Road, London, SW3 6RB
and Auckland, Melbourne, Singapore and Toronto

ISBN 0 600 57843 7

Produced by Mandarin Offset.
Printed and bound in Hong Kong

Editor: Isobel Holland
Art editor: Lisa Tai
Production controller: Sarah Rees
Picture researcher: Caroline Hensman
Jacket and Special photography: Clive Streeter

Contents

Basic Cakes

These cake recipes are used throughout the book. To make it easier to follow, the ingredients are set out in chart form with cake sizes indicated by numbers.

MADEIRA CAKE

Madeira cake has a moist texture, yet it doesn't crumble, and is firm enough for novelty cakes which require a lot of cutting and shaping.

PREPARATION TIME: about 15 minutes
COOKING TIME: see chart
OVEN: 160°C, 325°F, Gas mark 3

1 Grease the bakeware, line the base and sides with greaseproof paper and grease again.

2 Cream the butter and sugar until light, fluffy and very pale.

3 Sift the flours together. Beat the eggs into the creamed mixture, one at a time, following each with a spoonful of flour.

4 Fold the remaining flour into the creamed mixture, then add lemon rind.

5 Turn into the prepared bakeware and level the top. Bake in a preheated oven for the time suggested in the chart or until well risen, firm to the touch and golden brown.

6 Cool in the bakeware for about 10 minutes, then turn out on to a wire rack and leave until cold. Do not peel off the lining paper, but wrap the cake in foil or store in an airtight container for at least 12 hours before cutting.

Right: Madeira cake

MADEIRA CAKE

★ COMMUNAL SHOWER ★ ROMAN FANTASY ★ BATHTIME FUN ★ MALE STRIPPERS ★
★ BEDTIME WOES ★ MOTOR SHOW ★ LINGERIE ★

Size	20 x 10 cm (8 x 4 inch) OVAL BOWL 1	25 cm (10 inch) ROUND TIN 2	20 x 30 cm (8 x 12 inch) OBLONG TIN 3	25 cm (10 inch) SQUARE TIN 4	15 cm (6 inch) ROUND TIN 5
butter or margarine	225g (8oz)	275g (10oz)	350g (12oz)	350g (12oz)	175g (6oz)
caster sugar	225g (8oz)	275g (10oz)	350g (12oz)	350g (12oz)	175g (6oz)
self-raising flour	225g (8oz)	275g (10oz)	350g (12oz)	350g (12oz)	175g (6oz)
plain flour	125g (4oz)	150g (5oz)	175g (6oz)	175g (6oz)	75g (3oz)
eggs	4	5	6	6	3
grated lemon rind	1½ lemons	2 lemons	2 lemons	2 lemons	1 lemon
cooking time	1-1¼ hours	1-1¼ hours	1 hour	1-1¼ hours	1-1¼ hours

ℳADEIRA CAKE

★ OVER EXPOSED! ★ NUDIST BEACH ★ KISS ★ SCOTSMAN ★
★ RIDING THE WAVES ★

Size	2 x 8 cm (3½ inch) DIAMETER BOWLS 6	12 cm (5 inch) ROUND TIN 7	1.2 litre (2 pint) BOWL 8	20 cm (8 inch) ROUND TIN 9	25 cm (10 inch) HEART TIN 10
butter or margarine	50g (2oz)	50g (2oz)	150g (5oz)	175g (6oz)	275g (10oz)
caster sugar	50g (2oz)	50g (2oz)	150g (5oz)	175g (6oz)	275g (10oz)
self-raising flour	50g (2oz)	50g (2oz)	150g (5oz)	175g (6oz)	275g (10oz)
plain flour	25g (1oz)	25g (1oz)	65g (2½oz)	75g (3oz)	150g (5oz)
eggs (size 2 except *)	1	1	2* (size 1)	3	5
grated lemon rind	¼ lemon	¼ lemon	½ lemon	1 lemon	2 lemons
cooking time	35 minutes	45 minutes	1 hour	50 minutes	1-1¼ hours

VICTORIA SPONGE CAKE

A classic, light Victoria sponge mixture, which tastes extra rich when made with butter.

PREPARATION TIME: about 30 minutes
COOKING TIME: see chart
OVEN: 180°C, 375°F, Gas mark 4

1 Grease the bakeware and either dust with flour or line the base with greaseproof paper and grease again.

2 Cream the butter and sugar until light, fluffy and very pale, then beat in the vanilla flavouring.

3 Beat in the eggs, one at a time, following each with a spoonful of the self-raising flour.

4 Sift the remaining flour and fold it very gently into the mixture alternately with the water.

5 Turn into the prepared bakeware and level the top. Bake in a preheated oven for the time suggested in the chart or until well risen and firm to the touch. Turn out on to a wire rack and leave to cool.

QUICK MIX CAKE

This is a very simple cake to prepare and bake. It is moist and light but with a firm enough texture to allow for the cutting and shaping required for making novelty cakes.

PREPARATION TIME: about 5 minutes
COOKING TIME: see chart
OVEN: 160°C, 325°F, Gas mark 3

1 Grease the bakeware and dust with a little flour.

2 Put the butter, sugar, eggs, sifted flour, baking powder and vanilla flavouring into a large bowl.

3 Mix the ingredients together with a wooden spoon or hand-held electric mixer, then beat vigorously for 1-2 minutes until the mixture is smooth and glossy.

4 Turn the mixture into the prepared bakeware and level the top. Bake in a preheated oven for the time suggested in the chart, or until risen and firm to the touch.

5 Cool the cake in the bakeware for about 10 minutes, then turn out on to a wire rack.

6 When completely cold, store the cake in an airtight container or wrap it in foil and leave for at least 12 hours before cutting.

Right: Quick mix cake

V ICTORIA SPONGE CAKE

★ KAMA SUTRA ★ PARTY SURPRISE ★

SIZE	20 CM (8 INCH) ROUND TIN 1	12 CM (5 INCH) ROUND TIN 2	20 CM (8 INCH) SQUARE TIN 3
butter or margarine	350g (12oz)	125g (4oz)	225g (8oz)
caster sugar	350g (12oz)	125g (4oz)	225g (8oz)
vanilla flavouring	6 drops	2 drops	4 drops
eggs (size 1 or 2)	6	2	4
self-raising flour	350g (12oz)	125g (4oz)	225g (8oz)
cold water	1 tablespoon	2 teaspoons	1 tablespoon
cooking time	1¼ hours	45 minutes	50 minutes – 1 hour

QUICK MIX CAKE

★ BEDTIME WOES ★ BOOBS ★ WHOSE TURN ON TOP? ★ LINGERIE ★ MAID SERVICE! ★
★ ROMAN FANTASY ★ STRIP POKER! ★

SIZE	1.2 LITRE (2 PINT) BOWL 1	20 x 30 CM (8 x 12 INCH) OBLONG TIN 2	25 CM (10 INCH) SQUARE TIN 3	20 CM (8 INCH) SQUARE TIN 4
butter or margarine	175g (6oz)	350g (12oz)	275g (10oz)	275g (10oz)
caster sugar	175g (6oz)	350g (12oz)	275g (10oz)	275g (10oz)
eggs (size 1 or 2)	3	6	5	5
self-raising flour	175g (6oz)	350g (12oz)	275g (10oz)	275g (10oz)
baking powder	$1^{1}/_{2}$ teaspoons	3 teaspoons	$2^{1}/_{2}$ teaspoons	$2^{1}/_{2}$ teaspoons
vanilla flavouring	6 drops	12 drops	10 drops	10 drops
cooking time	$1-1^{1}/_{4}$ hours	1 hour	$1-1^{1}/_{4}$ hours	$1^{1}/_{4}$ hours

9

DEVIL'S FOOD CAKE

This is a wickedly rich chocolate and coffee cake which is moist, yet firm enough to cut into shapes.

PREPARATION TIME: 15 minutes
COOKING TIME: see chart
OVEN: 160°C, 325°F, Gas mark 3

1 Grease and line the bakeware with greaseproof paper, then grease again.

2 Make the coffee in a heat-resistant bowl. Add the chocolate drops and stir until melted. Leave to cool.

3 In a large bowl break up the butter or margarine with a fork, and then beat until soft. Add the soft dark brown sugar and the vanilla flavouring and beat the mixture until it is pale in colour and fluffy.

4 Gradually beat in the eggs, one at a time, then stir in the chocolate and coffee mixture.

5 Sift the plain flour and bicarbonate of soda together and gradually fold into the mixture a little at a time until well blended.

6 Stir in the soured cream.

7 Turn the mixture into the prepared bakeware and bake in a preheated oven for the time suggested in the chart, or until the cake is well risen and firm to the touch.

8 Leave the cake to cool for about 15 minutes, then turn out on to a wire rack. Do not peel off the lining paper, but wrap the cake in foil or store it in an airtight container for about 24 hours before cutting.

Right: Devil's food cake

D EVIL'S FOOD CAKE

★ HORNY LITTLE DEVIL ★ KAMA SUTRA ★ MUD WRESTLERS ★

	20 CM (8 INCH) SQUARE TIN	15 CM (6 INCH) ROUND TIN 1.2 LITRE (2 PINT) BOWL 2 x 8 CM (3½ INCH) DIAMETER BOWLS 7 CM (3 INCH) DIAMETER MUG
SIZE	1	2
hot, strong black coffee	175ml (6fl oz)	275ml (9fl oz)
plain chocolate drops	75g (3oz)	150g (5oz)
butter or margarine	175g (6oz)	250g (9oz)
soft dark brown sugar	275g (10oz)	425g (15oz)
vanilla flavouring	1 teaspoon	2 teaspoons
eggs	3 (size 2 or 3)	5 (size 3 or 4)
plain flour	275g (10oz)	425g (15oz)
bicarbonate of soda	1½ teaspoons	2 teaspoons
soured cream	175ml (6fl oz)	275ml (9fl oz)
cooking time	1–1¼ hours	15 cm (6 inch) – 1–1¼ hours 1.2 litre (2 pint) bowl – 1–1¼ hours 2 x 8 cm (3½ inch) – 35 minutes 7 cm (3 inch) mug – 35 minutes

For the Horny Little Devil cake, place 200g (7oz) of the mixture in the mug, 125g (4oz) in each small bowl, then divide the remaining mixture equally between the 15 cm (6 inch) round tin and the large ovenproof bowl. Put them in the oven together, removing the smaller cakes after the times stated in the chart, or when cooked.

LIGHT FRUIT CAKE

This moist, well-flavoured cake keeps for about 2 weeks in an airtight container. Alternatively, freeze it (before icing) for up to 3 months. If you like, replace the currants with chopped, stoned dates or no-need-to-soak dried apricots.

PREPARATION TIME: about 20 minutes
COOKING TIME: see chart
OVEN: 180°C, 350°F, Gas mark 4

1 Grease the bakeware, line the base with a double layer of greaseproof paper and grease again.

2 Sift the flour, bicarbonate of soda, spice and ginger into a bowl.

3 In another bowl, cream the butter and sugar until light, fluffy and pale.

4 Beat in the eggs, one at a time, following each with a spoonful of the flour mixture, then fold in the remaining flour.

5 Add the raisins, currants, sultanas, mixed peel, fruit rind and grated apple to the mixture and stir well until evenly blended.

6 Turn into the prepared bakeware and level the top. Bake in the centre of a preheated oven for the time suggested in the chart.

7 The cake is done when a skewer inserted into the centre comes out clean. Cool in the bakeware for about 10 minutes, then turn the cake out on to a wire rack and leave until cold. Do not peel off the lining paper, but wrap the cake in foil and freeze or store in an airtight container for 24-48 hours before cutting.

Variation: This light fruit cake as with any fruit cake can be adapted in many ways, for instance, the mixed spice could be replaced with a particular favourite such as cinnamon or nutmeg or cloves. The flavour of cloves is quite strong so reduce the quantity to $1/4$ teaspoon for both the cake sizes given. For a really tangy alternative, replace the orange or lemon rind with the rind of a lime, and once the cake has cooled, make a few deep holes using a fine skewer and add 3-4 teaspoons of dark rum. This would certainly lend an exotic flavour to your cake. Leave for 2-3 days before use.

ℒIGHT FRUIT CAKE

★ BOOBS ★ CAN CAN GIRL ★

SIZE	1.2 LITRE (2 PINT) BOWL 1	25 CM (10 INCH) ROUND TIN* 2
plain flour	175g (6oz)	225g (8oz)
bicarbonate of soda	$1/3$ teaspoon	$1/2$ teaspoon
mixed spice	$1/3$ teaspoon	$1/2$ teaspoon
ground ginger	good pinch	$1/4$ teaspoon
butter or margarine	125g (4oz)	175g (6oz)
light soft brown sugar	125g (4oz)	175g (6oz)
eggs	2 (size 3 or 4)	2 (size 1 or 2)
raisins	175g (6oz)	225g (8oz)
currants	75g (3oz)	125g (4oz)
sultanas	75g (3oz)	125g (4oz)
cut mixed peel	40g (1$1/2$oz)	50g (2oz)
grated orange or lemon rind	1 orange or lemon	1 orange or lemon
apple, grated	125g (4oz)	175g (6oz)
cooking time	1-1$1/4$ hours	50 minutes

*Bake this cake at a slight angle in the oven for the Can Can Girl cake

Right: Light fruit cake

RICH FRUIT CAKE

This recipe was given to me by my mother. It makes a deliciously dark and moist celebration cake.

PREPARATION TIME: 30 minutes
COOKING TIME: see chart
OVEN: 150°C, 300°F, Gas mark 2

1 Grease the cake tin, line with a double layer of greaseproof paper and grease again.

2 Quarter, wash and dry the cherries and place in a large bowl.

3 Add the sultanas, currants, raisins, mixed peel, ground almonds, chopped nuts, grated lemon rind and mixed spice. Mix well.

4 In another bowl, cream the butter and sugar until light, fluffy and pale.

5 Beat the eggs into the creamed mixture, one at a time, following each with a spoonful of the flour.

6 Add the black treacle.

7 Fold in the remaining flour and add the dried fruit mixture.

8 Turn the mixture into the prepared tin and level the top, then make a dip in the centre with the back of a spoon.

9 Tie a double layer of brown paper round the outside of the tin to protect the cake during cooking and place on a baking sheet lined with a double layer of brown paper.

10 Bake for the suggested cooking time and test by inserting a skewer into the centre. If it comes out clean the cake is done. If not, return to the oven for about 10 minutes more and then check again.

11 Leave the cake to cool in the tin. When cold, remove from the tin and wrap in greaseproof paper, then in foil. A final wrap of clingfilm will help keep the cake moist during storage.

12 To improve the flavour, pierce the cake with a skewer and spoon several tablespoons of brandy over it.

Variation: If you would like to make this cake a little lighter in colour, replace the black treacle with 1 tablespoon of golden syrup and replace the soft brown sugar with 225g (8oz) caster sugar.

Note: Although this cake is at its best 3 months after baking, eating it before doesn't matter at all. However, until you are ready to eat it, keep in an airtight container.

Right: Rich fruit cake

RICH FRUIT CAKE

★ PARTY SURPRISE ★

	20 CM (8 INCH) ROUND TIN & 12 CM (5 INCH) ROUND TIN
currants	350g (12oz)
sultanas	500g (1lb 2oz)
raisins	175g (6oz)
glacé cherries	175g (6oz)
cut mixed peel	75g (3oz)
mixed chopped nuts	75g (3oz)
ground almonds	75g (3oz)
grated lemon rind	2 lemons
plain flour	400g (14oz)
mixed spice	2 teaspoons
butter	350g (12oz)
soft brown sugar	350g (12oz)
eggs (size 2)	6
black treacle	2 tablespoons
cooking time	20 cm (8 inch) tin – 4 hours 12 cm (5 inch) tin – 2¾ hours

Fill the larger tin with 1.95kg (4lb 5oz) of the mixture and put the remaining 750g (1lb 11oz) in the smaller tin. Put them in the oven together, removing the smaller cake after 2¾ hours, or when cooked.

Icings and Fillings

The following recipes include all the icings and fillings you will need throughout the book. For instructions on how to colour icing, see page 23.

FONDANT ICING

Fondant icing (sugarpaste) can be bought from cake decorating suppliers, supermarkets and other outlets. Some brands are easier to use than others, so it is best to try a few to find the one you work with best. The ready-made icing is usually of high quality, but if you prefer to make your own, here is the recipe. As a general rule, this icing is rolled to a thickness of 3 mm (¹/₈ inch) before use.

MAKES 675g (1¹/₂lb)
1 egg white
2 tablespoons liquid glucose
675g (1¹/₂lb) icing sugar, sifted
a little white fat (optional)

1 Put the egg white and liquid glucose into a bowl and gradually add the icing sugar. Stir until the mixture thickens.

2 Turn out on to a surface dusted with icing sugar and knead until the paste is smooth and silky. If the paste becomes a little dry and cracked, try kneading in a little white fat.

PASTILLAGE ICING

A pastillage mix, in powder form, can be obtained from cake decorating suppliers. If you prefer to make your own, here is a recipe to try. This icing is suitable for making precision sugar items such as the lid for the Boxed Lingerie cake on page 29 and the bedhead in Bedtime Woes on page 83, as it dries so hard.

MAKES 350g (12oz)
1 teaspoon powdered egg white
25 ml (1fl oz) water
2 teaspoons powdered gelatine
1 teaspoon liquid glucose
350g (12oz) icing sugar, sifted

1 In a clean bowl, mix the powdered egg white with half of the water, gradually adding a little at a time and stirring thoroughly.

2 Pour the remaining water into a

Left: Fondant icing is made by combining egg white, liquid glucose and icing sugar into a thick and malleable mixture.

Below: It is best to thoroughly knead fondant icing until it is soft and pliable.

Above: Royal icing is useful for piping and styling hair and sticking modelled items together.

Left: Figures made from modelling fondant.

separate bowl and sprinkle on the gelatine powder. Leave for a few moments, then place the bowl over a pan of hot water. As soon as the gelatine has dissolved completely, gently stir in the liquid glucose, then add the egg white mixture. Add about three-quarters of the sifted icing sugar, a little at a time, and stir with a spoon until the mixture thickens.

3 Turn the mixture out on to a work surface that has been liberally dusted with icing sugar. Knead thoroughly, gradually incorporating the remaining icing sugar.

4 Wrap the icing in a polythene bag and store in an airtight container for up to 2 weeks.

MODELLING FONDANT

This is fondant icing with gum tragacanth added. It makes the icing firmer and easy to shape into figures, animals and small objects but, once it is unwrapped, you have to work quickly as it starts to dry after a few minutes. Gum tragacanth is available in powder form from cake decorating suppliers and some chemists.

MAKES 450g (1lb)
2 teaspoons gum tragacanth
450g (1lb) fondant icing

1 Put the gum tragacanth on a clean surface and knead into the fondant. Wrap in a polythene bag and leave for about 8 hours before use to allow the gum to take effect.

ROYAL ICING

When I first started cake decorating I was terrified of piping with royal icing and avoided it as long as I could, but once I started, I realized just how simple it really is. With a little practice, you will too. A few tips to bear in mind are as follows. To achieve a good, glossy finish on royal icing it is essential to have everything spotlessly clean and as dust-free as possible, little dust particles have a habit of coming to the surface once the icing is set. Once the icing has been made, make sure you cover it as soon as possible to exclude all the air and prevent it from drying out before you use it.

See pages 22 and 24 to find out how to fold a paper piping bag.

MAKES ABOUT 225g (8oz)
1 egg white
1 teaspoon lemon juice
225-250g (8-9oz) icing sugar, sifted

1 Put the egg white and lemon juice into a bowl and beat in the icing sugar, a little at a time, until the icing is smooth, white, and forms soft peaks when the spoon is pulled out.

2 Cover the bowl with a damp cloth and leave to stand for 5 minutes to disperse any air bubbles before use. Store in an airtight container in the refrigerator for up to 10 days.

MARZIPAN

Ready-made marzipan or almond paste is widely available, especially at Christmas, but if you make your own you can vary the colour. For a white marzipan, replace the egg with 2 egg whites; for a brighter yellow version, use 2 egg yolks.

MAKES 450g (1lb)
125g (4oz) icing sugar, sifted
125g (4oz) caster sugar
225g (8oz) ground almonds
1 egg, lightly beaten
1 teaspoon lemon juice
few drops of almond essence

1 Put the sugars and almonds into a bowl. Add the egg, lemon juice and almond essence and mix together until it forms a stiff dough.

2 Turn out on to a surface dusted with icing sugar and knead until smooth. Wrap the marzipan in a polythene bag and store for 2-3 days.

APRICOT GLAZE

This is best made shortly before you need it. It can be made up to a week ahead and stored in an airtight container in the refrigerator, but it will have to be boiled and cooled again before using.

MAKES 150ml (¼pint)
150g (5oz) apricot jam
2-3 tablespoons water

1 Put the jam and water into a saucepan and heat gently, stirring occasionally, until the jam melts. Simmer gently for 1-2 minutes.

2 Rub through a sieve and allow to cool slightly before using.

Variation: Although apricot jam probably makes the best glaze for use between the cake and the icing, raspberry jam may be used, too, but should only be used on cakes with dark icing as it can show through pale colours.

LEMON CURD

Lemon curd is ideal to use instead of apricot glaze on the light fruit cake or any of the sponge cakes. You can use the bought variety if you don't have time to make your own, but this recipe below is easy to make and tastes delicious. Once made it can be stored for up to 1 month in a cool place or for up to 3 months in a refrigerator.

MAKES ABOUT 675g (1½lb)
225g (8oz) sugar cubes
3-4 large lemons
125g (4oz) unsalted butter
5 eggs, beaten

1 Rub the sugar cubes on the rind of the lemons until they are well-coloured and have absorbed the zest of the fruit.

2 Squeeze the juice from the lemons, there should be approximately 400ml (14fl oz), if not squeeze another lemon.

3 Heat the butter slowly in a heavy-based pan until it has melted, then add the sugar cubes and lemon juice and carry on heating gently until the sugar has dissolved. Do not allow to boil.

4 In a large bowl, stir 1 tablespoon of the hot mixture into the beaten eggs, repeat twice more. This helps to prevent eggs curdling.

5 Pour the mixture back into the pan and heat gently, stirring with a wooden spoon, until the mixture thickens and coats the back of a wooden spoon. Do not allow to boil.

6 Pour into hot sterilized jars and cover.

Variation: This recipe is easily adaptable for oranges to make a tasty alternative.

Left: Marzipan; apricot glaze

BUTTER CREAM

Butter cream is easy to work with and has many uses when making novelty cakes.

MAKES 350g (12oz)
125g (4oz) butter or soft margarine
225g (8oz) icing sugar, sifted
few drops of vanilla flavouring
1-2 tablespoons milk or water

1 Place the butter or soft magarine in a bowl and cream together until very soft.

2 Gradually beat in the icing sugar, adding vanilla to taste, and just enough milk or water to give a firm but spreadable consistency. If not using straightway, store in an airtight container in the refrigerator for up to 1 week. Allow to return to room temperature before using.

VARIATION: Chocolate Butter Cream
Dissolve 1-2 tablespoons sifted cocoa powder in a little hot water to give a thin paste. Allow to cool slightly before beating into the butter cream in place of the milk.

CONTINENTAL BUTTER CREAM

A deliciously rich, smooth butter cream for sandwiching cakes together.

MAKES ABOUT 275g (10oz)
75g (3oz) caster sugar
4 tablespoons water
2 egg yolks
175g (6oz) unsalted butter

1 Put the sugar and water into a small, heavy-based saucepan and heat gently until the sugar dissolves completely.

2 Put a sugar thermometer into the pan, bring up to the boil, and then boil steadily for 2-3 minutes, until the syrup reaches 110°C, 225°F. If you do not have a sugar thermometer, try the thread test: dip the back of a teaspoon into the syrup and pull the syrup away with the back of another spoon. It should form a thin thread. If this does not happen, boil for another minute and test again.

3 Put the egg yolks into a large bowl and whisk well (a hand-held electric mixer is best, but a balloon or rotary whisk will do). Whisking constantly, pour the syrup in a thin stream on to the yolks (not on to the mixer or bowl). Continue whisking until the mixture is thick and cool.

4 In another bowl, cream the butter until soft and light, then beat in the egg yolk mixture a little at a time, until smooth and spreadable.

Above left: Continental butter cream; above right: butter cream.

Equipment and Techniques

The following information outlines equipment and techniques that are useful to both the beginner and practised cake maker.

There are hundreds of items you can buy to help with cake decorating, but if you are not an avid cake maker and decorator and only make cakes when the need arises, there are plenty of items from your kitchen cupboards that you can use instead of going out and breaking the bank!

For baking the cakes, different containers such as ovenproof bowls and mugs can be put to excellent use. For any circles that need to be cut, instead of using special plain circle cutters, as a guide to cut around you can use cups, mugs and egg-cups of the required size.

For decorating cakes, a sharp knife, a rolling pin and a few cocktail sticks are essential, but the rest you can improvise with items from your kitchen.

Cake boards

Cake boards come in a variety of shapes and sizes and are usually covered in silver foil, although gold and metallic red are obtainable. To make your cake look even better, I recommend you cover the board with fondant icing. Alternatively you can use colour co-ordinating paper, as long as it is greaseproof. Glue the paper to the cake board with a mixture of 2 teaspoons flour mixed to a paste with a few drops of water. Brush thinly on to the surface of the board using a pastry brush, cover with the paper, then leave to dry.

Greaseproof paper piping bags

These can be purchased ready-made in small and large sizes, but a triangular shape cut from a sheet of greaseproof paper or baking parchment will fold just as well (see pages 22 and 24).

Piping nozzles

I recommend that you use good quality piping nozzles, which, although more expensive, do last a lifetime. The basic writing nozzles in sizes 1–4 are used in this book for piping royal icing and indenting shapes using both ends.

Small rolling pin

This is useful for rolling out small pieces of fondant icing as a large rolling pin can be quite clumsy.

Turntable

For easy access to all sides of the cake you are working on, I recommend you

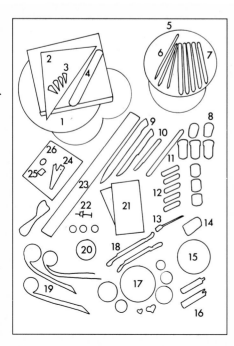

The following list is a guide to some of the useful items available from cake decorating suppliers (see page 86).

1 Cake boards
2 Greaseproof piping bags
3 Piping nozzles
4 Small rolling pin
5 Turntable
6 Paintbrushes
7 Food colouring pens
8 Food colouring pastes
9 Knives
10 Craft knife
11 Wooden and plastic skewers (dowelling)
12 Powder colours
13 Miniature brush
14 Gum arabic
15 Garrett frill cutter
16 Crimping tools
17 Basic cutters
18 Modelling tools
19 Ribbons
20 Pins
21 Smoother with handle
22 Plunger and blossom cutters
23 Ruler
24 Cocktail sticks
25 Embossing stamps
26 Foam

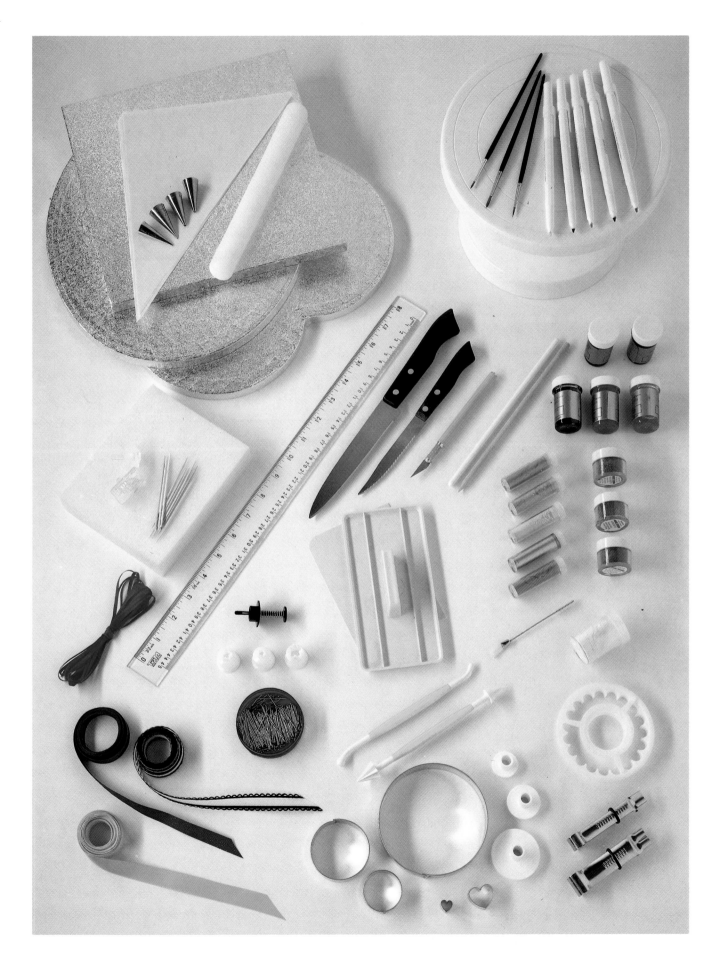

1 *Fold a square of greaseproof paper in half diagonally and roll into a cone.*

2 *Fold the two extending points into the cone, secure with tape if necessary.*

use a turntable. The one shown here is metal, which can be expensive, but cheaper plastic ones are obtainable. If you prefer, use an upturned tin.

Paintbrushes

I recommend that you use good quality sable paintbrushes as they do not shed hairs like the cheaper versions. The basic sizes shown here should be enough to start.

Food colouring pens

These are felt tip pens filled with food colouring and come in a rainbow of colours and are extremely useful. Always use them after the icing has dried as the colour can spread.

Food colouring pastes

These come in a vast range of colours, but the basic primaries, red, blue, yellow and black are all you need to start with as you can mix these to achieve different colours.

Knives

To help with your cake decorating, make sure you have good sharp knives to work with in a variety of sizes.

Craft knife

Very useful for cutting out small pieces of fondant. Replacement blades can be purchased.

Wooden and plastic skewers (dowelling)

These are used to help support the cakes that stand quite high. I have also used them for the Nudist Beach parsol (see page 74) and the wrestling ring in the Mud Wrestlers cake (see page 63).

Powder colours

These come in a variety of colours, plain or lustre. Brushed on with a dry paintbrush, they give just a hint of colour or sparkle, but can be quite messy to use. You can also mix them to a paste with a few drops of clear alcohol or water for painting on dry icing, which is especially effective with the silver and gold lustre powders.

Miniature brush

Very helpful in brushing away any loose icing sugar left on the cake and as it is so small, it will get to any awkward corner.

Gum arabic

Available from any cake decorating supplier, this white powder is used as a glue to stick items on to cakes. Mix together a small amount with a few drops of water.

Garrett frill cutter

This garrett frill cutter has a removable inner circle so you can use other circle cutters to change the depth of the frill (see page 25 on how to make a garrett frill).

Crimping tools

These are available in many shapes and are used to make patterns by gently pinching the fondant icing together. It is often used to create a decorative border on the fondant icing-covered cake board.

Basic cutters

There are many special cutters which are available in different sizes and designs. A basic set of plastic or metal circle cutters are especially useful.

Modelling tools

These can work out to be expensive items. However, children's plastic craft tools available from toy and craft shops work out much cheaper and do the job just as well.

Ribbons

Ribbons with co-ordinating colours and patterns for the cake board banding, add the finishing touch to your cake. Remember, if you are going to ice the board, you will need a slightly wider ribbon than if you do not. A pin to hold the ribbon in place at the back of the board can be disguised with a small ribbon bow.

Pins

Pins are used to hold the ribbon banding in place on the cake board. They can also be used to make small marks or patterns on the icing.

Smoother with handle

This is used for smoothing out any dents in the icing to get a good finish. To use the smoother see page 24.

Plunger and blossom cutters

These blossom cutters attach to the end of the plunger and when used, make a prettily-shaped flower with an indented centre. When making the blossoms always push out on to a piece of foam as this helps to give shape to the flower and they also dry more quickly. A variety of different shapes can be bought to attach to the plunger, such as a bow shape.

Ruler

Used for any accurate measuring required, but also for any straight line you wish to mark into the fondant icing.

Cocktail sticks

These are used to add colour to the icing (see below), and they have no end of uses when making modelled items or marking details on a cake.

Embossing stamps

These are designs with a raised outline, which when pushed gently into fondant icing, make an impression.

Foam

Your modelling work dries much quicker if placed on a piece of foam, as the air can circulate underneath as well as above. Foam is also used when making plunger flowers, as the centre of each flower is pressed into the foam to give it more shape.

Additional equipment, not illustrated, but which can be useful, includes the following:

Spacers

These are long narrow strips of plastic that help the fondant icing roll out evenly, which is particularly useful when rolling out large pieces.

Polythene bags

Essential for storing fondant or pastillage icing after it has been coloured. Don't put different colours together in the same bag, as strong colours will 'bleed' into others.

Voile netting

A small piece of this material is always useful to have as you can create a pretty pattern by gently pushing the netting into the icing, see page 56.

Large rolling pin

Essential for rolling out large pieces of fondant icing. The plastic made ones are much the best.

I recommend you use the paste or concentrated liquid food colouring obtainable from cake decorating suppliers. The liquid form sold in most supermarkets can make your icing too wet, especially if you have to achieve a deep colour. However, it is fine if only a pale shade is required.

Powdered food colouring can be quite messy, so it is best to use it only for dusting on when the icing is dry to achieve just a hint of colour. Edible gold and silver powder can be painted on to the icing after mixing with a few drops of clear alcohol.

Food colouring pens come in many shades and avoid the need for paintbrushes. Only use the pens on icing that has had at least a day to dry out and before you start, brush off any excess icing sugar from the surface to prevent the food colouring from spreading out. If these pens aren't available, you can paint on the dry icing using concentrated food colouring that has been watered down to a watercolour paint consistency. Again, thoroughly brush off any loose icing sugar to prevent the colour from spreading.

How to colour fondant

Put a little colour on the end of a cocktail stick and add to the fondant. Fold it in and knead thoroughly until the colour is even throughout, with no streaks. If you want a deep colour, add more food colouring a little at a time to achieve the required shade.

How to colour royal icing

Put a little colour on the end of a cocktail stick, add to the icing and stir. You will find that this icing takes colour easily and a bright colour such as red can get brighter, so leave the icing covered with a damp cloth for a few minutes for the colour to develop.

How to roll out fondant

Take the required amount of fondant and knead it a little to warm it up. Dust

Above: Rolling out fondant icing

the surface liberally with icing sugar to prevent the paste from sticking. Press the fondant on to the icing sugar, turn over and press again, then roll out the fondant, moving it around frequently so that it doesn't stick to the surface. Continue rolling out until it is about 3 mm ($^1/_8$ inch) thick.

Gold and silver colouring

Gold leaf is difficult to use and very expensive, but most effective when applied to fondant. Always use as manufacturer's instructions, or paint a very thin layer of clear piping gel on the surface of the fondant first as an adhesive.

Gold lustre powder is not so 'gold' looking when mixed with liquid and painted on the fondant, but looks very effective when the dry powder is brushed over the surface of the fondant to give a sparkle.

Gold liquid is obtainable from cake decorating suppliers and although easy to use, is inedible. This must only be used on decorations that are to be removed and not eaten.

Silver lustre powder is the only silver colour you need to use. Mixed with a little clear alcohol, it is very effective and also edible, although it has a slightly metallic taste. If brushed dry on to the surface of the fondant it gives a sparkle, although it can make the fondant look a little grey. There is also a brilliant silver lustre powder obtainable.

Helpful Hints

The following tips are intended to give helpful advice and practical information to instructions that arise throughout this book.

How to smooth a cake surface

Cake smoothers are invaluable, as your hands alone will not get a perfect surface. They are relatively cheap and are available from cake decorating suppliers. The cake smoother with a handle is best for novelty cakes as it has rounded edges. Rub the surface of the cake in a circular motion, pressing quite firmly to remove any dents in the fondant.

Joins in the fondant should be removed before the icing starts to dry by rubbing with your fingers in a circular motion.

How to stick pieces of fondant together

A little water applied with a fine paintbrush will stick fondant icing together, but it is not strong enough for large pieces or for your modelling fondant figures. I recommend you use a little egg white or gum arabic, which is an edible glue available in powder form from cake decorating suppliers.

How to make a piping bag

Cut a 25 cm (10 inch) square of greaseproof paper or baking parchment and fold in half diagonally, then roll into a

cone with two points extending at the top. Holding the base of the cone like an ice cream, fold the two points into the cone. Snip the point off and insert the nozzle. If you have a lot of piping to do, you may like to make the bag extra secure with a piece of tape.

How to cover a cake board with fondant icing

Roll out the fondant icing. Dampen the cake board with a little water, then place the icing on the board and smooth with a cake smoother to get a completely flat surface. Trim the edges with a sharp knife.

How to use confectioners glaze

To produce a soft sheen on the surface of the fondant, paint on a thin layer of the glaze using a paintbrush. For a shine, allow the surface to dry thoroughly, then apply a further thin layer. Available from cake decorating suppliers, see page 86.

How to grease and line a baking tin or ovenproof bowl

Place the cake tin on to a sheet of clean greaseproof paper and mark the outline with a pencil. Cut around the outline using a pair of sharp scissors. To measure the sides of the tin, take a piece of string and wrap it round the outside, use this to cut out another piece of greaseproof paper. Melt a little butter or margarine in a saucepan,

Left: Lining a cake tin

How to make a garret frill

1 *Thinly roll out fondant icing, cut with a garret frill cutter or fluted and plain cutters.*

2 *Gently roll the end of a cocktail stick dipped in cornflour over each loop until the icing becomes thin and starts to frill. Cut open frilled circle, stick on cake with a little water.*

then brush a thin coat on to the inside of the tin. Position both the cut-out base and sides inside the tin. Brush another thin layer of grease over the paper.

If you need to line an ovenproof bowl, cut a small circle out of grease-proof paper, large enough to cover the base only. Brush the inside of the bowl with melted fat, then position the paper in the bottom of the bowl.

Cornelli work
To create this lacy-effect pattern, use a small plain piping nozzle and pipe erratic 'W' and 'M' shapes. Depending on the thickness or boldness required use Nos. 1–4. Do not overfill the piping bag with royal icing as it may come out of the top. Fill halfway and re-fill 2 or 3 times as you are working.

ℱACTS AND FIGURES

- Unless otherwise stated, all spoon measurements given in this book are level.

- All eggs are size 2 unless otherwise stated.

- Both metric and imperial measurements have been calculated separately. Use one set of measurements only as they are not exact equivalents. In some recipes, you may find an apparent discrepancy in the metric equivalents. This is done to ensure a correct proportion of ingredients.

- Cooking times may vary slightly depending on the individual oven. Cakes should be placed in the centre of the oven unless otherwise specified. Always preheat the oven to the specified temperature.

- All icing is assumed to be coloured before you start following the recipe and all basic cakes baked. For detailed instructions on how to colour all kinds of icing see page 23.

- All icing used should be rolled to a thickness of 3 mm/⅛ inch unless otherwise stated.

- All skewers in the text refer to plastic or wooden dowelling that can be bought from hardware stores and specialist cake decorating suppliers.

- It may sometimes be necessary to use cocktail sticks to support heads on figures, but always warn your guests first.

Horny Little Devil

If your favourite hellraiser is feeling his years, perk him up with a wicked birthday cake.

YOU WILL NEED:

5 devil's food cakes (size 2)
2.25kg (4lb 14oz) fondant icing
black, red, orange and brown food colouring paste
400g (14oz) chocolate butter cream
egg white or gum arabic

EQUIPMENT:

5–6 cocktail sticks
25 cm (10 inch) round cake board
medium heart cutter
skewer or dowelling
fine paintbrush

COLOUR:

Fondant icing: 675g (1lb 6oz) black, 1.57kg (3lb 7³/₄oz) rusty red (red with a touch of orange and brown), 5g (¹/₄oz) white

1 Cover the cake board with 250g (9oz) of the black fondant. Using the heart cutter, cut out heart shapes all round the edge of the board, then set aside and leave to dry.

2 Slice the tops off all the cakes so they are completely flat, then cut the mug cake into 3 equal slices. Cut one of the slices into quarters. Trim the remaining 2 circles to make oval shapes for the feet; trim off any angles.

3 Place the large bowl cake on top of the 15 cm (6 inch) round cake. To mark the arms, make a cut about 1 cm (¹/₂ inch) deep, and continue to cut in a curving line down to the bottom of the bowl cake. Mark the back of the arm with a similar curving line 5 cm (2 inches) behind the first line. Repeat for the other arm, but make the curve slightly higher.

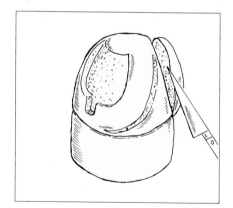

4 Slice down the front, keeping the tummy area quite rounded, and trim round to the arms. Slice downwards at the back, keeping the bottom area rounded, then trim round to the arms.

5 Slice out a piece of cake directly underneath each arm, then trim the base of the cake by about 5 mm (¹/₄ inch) all the way round, cutting at an inwards angle. Trim the edges off the arms and trim any angles left round the cake.

6 Sandwich the 2 cakes together with 125g (4oz) of the butter cream, then place on the cake board.

7 To make the head, sandwich the 2 small bowl cakes together with some butter cream. Trim the front almost flat to shape the face.

8 Stick the 2 feet in position with a little butter cream, then stick 1 of the small cake quarters on top of each foot for the legs, the right angle forming the knees.

9 Spread a thin layer of butter cream all over the cakes to help the fondant stick and prevent crumbs.

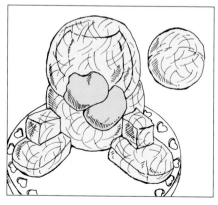

10 With 2 40g (1¹/₂oz) pieces of the rusty red fondant, model the hands and stick in position.

26

11 Roll a 20g (³/₄oz) ball for the nose and 2 very thin sausage shapes for the eyebrows. Stick on the face cake.

12 Roll out 850g (1lb 14oz) of the rusty red fondant, lift carefully and place over the body, smoothing down to shape. Don't worry if the back becomes untidy, as this will be covered later by the black cloak.

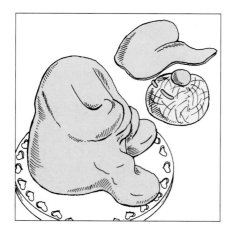

13 Roll out 225g (8oz) of the rusty red fondant and use to cover the front of the head, smoothing carefully over the facial features. Mark the devil's wicked grin with a knife.

14 Place the head on the body and push the skewer or dowelling down through the top of the head to keep it fixed firmly in place.

15 Model the ears, pointed at the top, with 2 5g (¹/₄oz) pieces of the rusty red fondant. Make the 2 top horns with 5g (¹/₄oz) each, and the 2 side horns with 10g (¹/₂oz) each.

16 Cover the back of the head with 100g (3¹/₂oz) of the rusty red fondant and pinch with your fingers for the hair. Using 150g (5oz), model the side-burns, the beard and the hair in front of the horns and stick in place with a little egg white or gum arabic.

17 Model the heart-shaped tail end with 75g (3oz) of the rusty red fondant and set aside to dry.

18 Roll out the remaining rusty red fondant with the trimmings and cut hearts with the heart cutter. Slot in all round the edge of the cake board.

19 With the white fondant, model the eyes and stick in place with a little egg white or gum arabic.

20 With a small amount of the black fondant, make the pupils for the eyes and the eyebrows and stick in place.

21 Roll a long smooth sausage shape with 100g (3¹/₂oz) of the black fondant and stick it in place round the devil to act as his tail. Place a small piece at the top of his hands, and position the heart-shaped tail end on top of this, securing it with a little egg white or gum arabic.

22 For the devil's cloak, roll out the remaining black fondant and cut a neat oblong shape which measures at least 15 x 25 cm (6 x 10 inches), tapering in slightly at the top. Stick the cloak in place around the back of the devil and roll the top down slightly to make the collar.

23 Leave the cake to dry for at least 8 hours, or overnight to allow the icing to set firmly.

Alternative designs:

This cheeky little devil can easily be turned into a more colourful little fella by altering his colour scheme. You could colour his cloak a deep midnight blue and his body a bright red. If this cake is for a special person, make the heart at the end of the tail really stand out by painting it gold or silver, and maybe even writing a saucy message on it. See page 23 for using gold or silver and use a food colouring pen of your choice for the message.

Boxed Lingerie

A birthday cake for the friend who's got everything — including the perfect figure.

𝒴ou will need:

1 Madeira cake (size 4) or quick
   mix cake (size 3)
1.125kg (2lb 8oz) fondant icing
500g (1lb 2oz) modelling fondant
275g (10oz) pastillage mix or
   350g (12oz) pastillage icing
125g (4oz) royal icing
black food colouring paste
225g (8oz) butter cream
1 tablespoon liquid glucose
silver lustre powder
2 teaspoons clear alcohol, eg vodka
   or gin

𝓔quipment:

30 cm (12 inch) square cake
   board
1-2 cocktail sticks
ruler
No. 3 piping nozzle
broderie eyelet cutter
fine paintbrush
3 ribbon bows
ribbon

𝒞olour:

Fondant icing: 350g (12oz) black,
   800g (1lb 12oz) white
Modelling fondant: 300g (11oz)
   white, 200g (7oz) black
Pastillage mix: 275g (10oz) white or
   Pastillage icing: 350g (12oz) white
Royal icing: 125g (4oz) white

1 Cover the cake board with the black fondant icing and leave to dry.

2 Slice the top off the cake so it is completely flat.

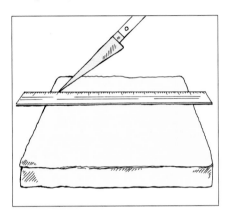

3 To make an oblong box shape, cut a strip measuring 6–7 cm (2½-3 inches) from one side of the cake.

4 Spread a layer of butter cream all over the cake to help the fondant stick. Place the cake on the cake board at a slight angle.

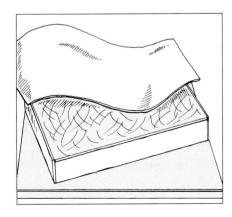

5 Roll out the white fondant icing and measure and cut pieces to fit the 4 sides and the top of the cake. Keep the edges and corners as precise as you can, so when the pastillage icing sides are in place they sit straight.

6 To make the box sides, measure the sides of the cake, allowing for the corners. As pastillage icing crusts so quickly, roll out and cut one side at a time, keeping the rest in a sealed polythene bag. Roll out the icing as thin as a sheet of card and make each box side 7 cm (3 inch) deep. Leave to dry on a completely flat surface.

7 To make the lid, measure the top of the cake and add about 5 mm (¼ inch) to each measurement to allow for the overlap. Roll out 150g (5oz) of the pastillage mix or 175g (6oz) of the pastillage icing and cut to size. Again, leave to dry on a completely flat surface.

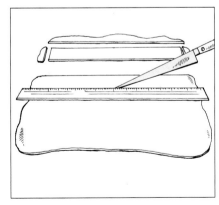

8 With the remaining pastillage icing, cut 4 strips 2.5 cm (1 inch) deep to fit the sides of the box lid. Leave all the pastillage pieces to dry completely for 24 hours, or slightly longer for the home-made recipe.

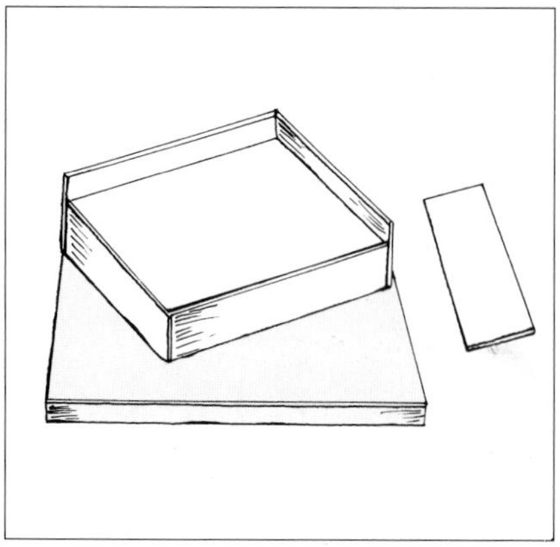

9 When the pastillage pieces are dry, stick the box sides in place using the royal icing and the No. 3 piping nozzle. Fill any gaps at the corners with a little of the white royal icing smoothed into them.

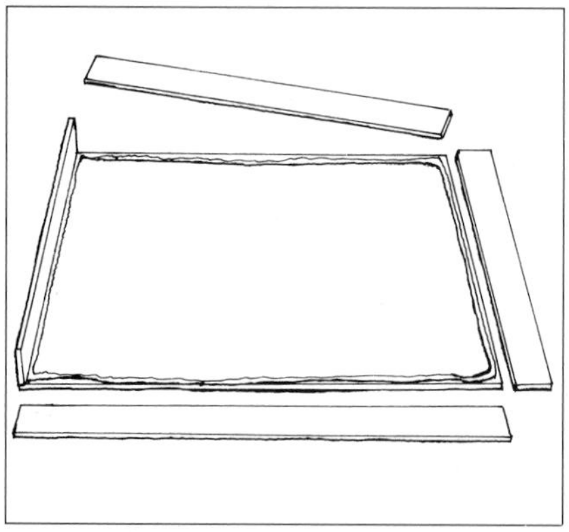

10 Assemble the box lid by piping royal icing along each edge, then pressing the side strips in place. If you find they need a little support while drying, try pushing the side of a book up against them.

11 To make the tissue paper, knead the liquid glucose into the white modelling fondant. (This will make the tissue movable, so you can cover the cake with the lid for presentation.) Roll out and cut an oblong measuring 23 x 38 cm (9 x 15 inches). Lift gently and place in the box, letting it fold naturally.

12 To make the basque, roll out the black modelling fondant and cut out the basque shape. Carefully cut out 4 shaped holes down the centre. Using

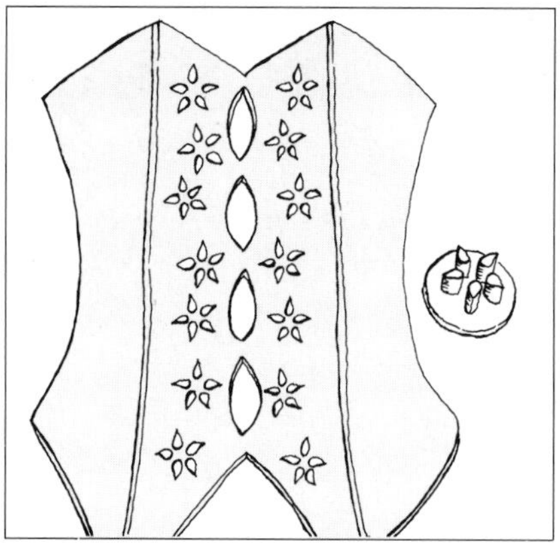

a knife, mark the decorative lines on either side. Cut out the flowery pattern using the broderie eyelet cutter. Fold the basque into the box.

13 Mix the silver lustre powder to a paste with the clear alcohol. Using a fine paintbrush, paint tiny dots over the tissue paper and larger dots on the box sides and the lid.

14 Secure the 3 bows in place with a little royal icing. Cut the 2 straps from the ribbon and tuck the ends under the top of the basque.

15 Leave the cake to dry for at least 8 hours, or overnight.

Right: Boxed lingerie

Alternative design:

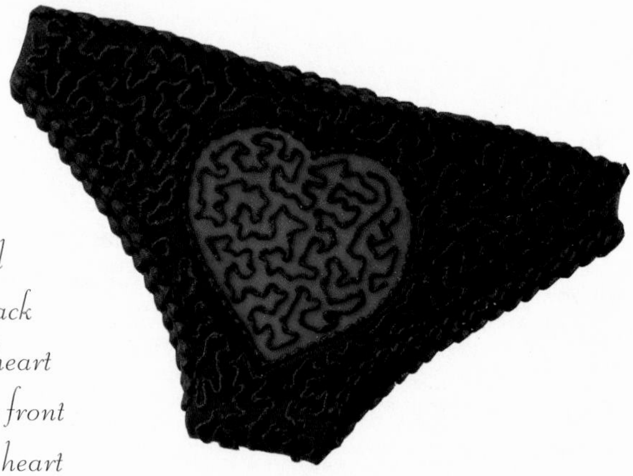

Instead of making a basque try your hand at a pair of black panties. Roll out 50g (2oz) of black modelling fondant and cut out the front and back of the panties. Cut a heart from the centre of the front part, using a large heart cutter, and fill the space with a heart cut from red modelling fondant, rolled slightly thinner. Stick in place with a little egg white or gum arabic, then fold the panties over, sticking the two sides together. With 25g (1oz) of black royal icing and a No. 2 piping nozzle, pipe small dots around the edge of the heart. Pipe cornelli work all over, then pipe larger dots around the edge to make the panties look even more lacy.

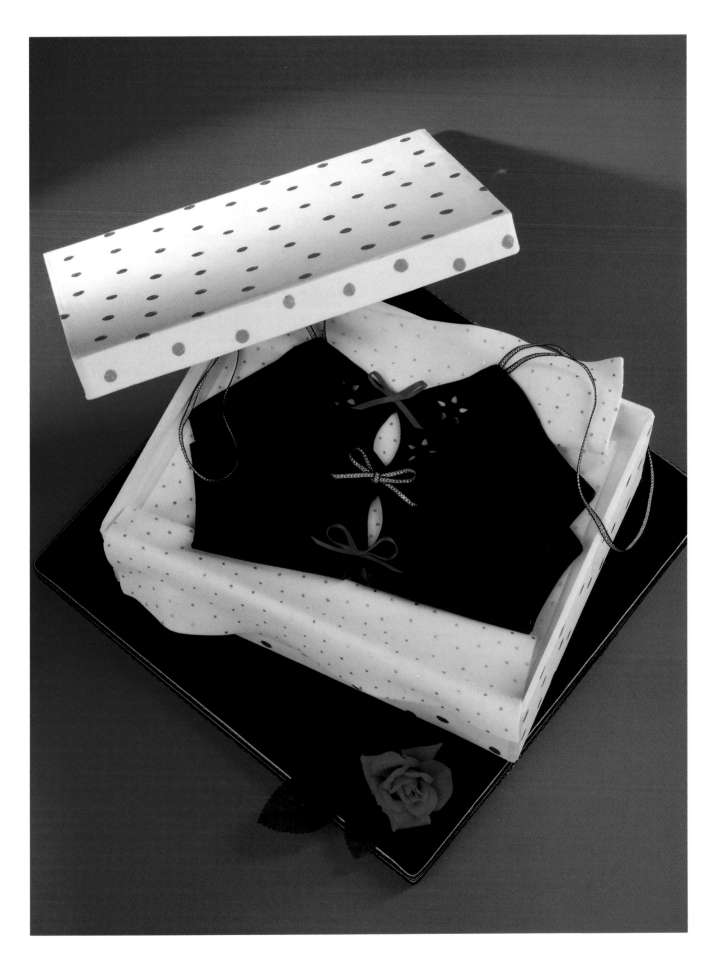

Male Strippers

These naughty boys with a saucy glint in their eyes will go down a treat for a girls' night out (or in).

You will need:

1 Madeira cake (size 2)
1.275kg (2lb 13oz) fondant icing
750g (1lb 11oz) modelling fondant
175g (6oz) royal icing
black, flesh, brown, egg yellow and red food colouring paste
egg white or gum arabic
225g (8oz) butter cream
white edible glitter
silver lustre powder
2 teaspoons clear alcohol, eg vodka or gin
black food colouring pen

Equipment:

7–8 cocktail sticks
30 cm (12 inch) round cake board
25 cm (10 inch) square cake board
small, medium and large star cutters
fine paintbrush
foam sheet
Nos. 1, 2 and 3 piping nozzles
narrow silver ribbon

Colour:

Fondant icing: 600g (1lb 5oz) black, 675g (1lb 8oz) white
Modelling fondant: 150g (5oz) flesh, 40g (1½oz) brown, 40g (1½oz) dark brown, 525g (1lb 3oz) white
Royal icing: 25g (1oz) cream (a touch of egg yellow), 25g (1oz) brown, 15g (½oz) red/brown, 40g (1½oz) black, 25g (1oz) white, 25g (1oz) red

1 Cover the 2 cake boards with the black fondant. Indent the star pattern all over both boards using the small, medium and large star cutters. Set aside and leave to dry.

2 Each stripper is made with about 40g (1½oz) of modelling fondant, using 5g (¼oz) for the head and a tiny nose, the rest for the body. To make each body, roll a sausage shape and cut half way down for the legs. Cut the arms at the sides, then shape the bodies in different poses, as shown above. Model 6 strippers, 4 with the flesh-coloured fondant, 1 with the brown and 1 with the dark brown. Carefully mark their mouths with a cocktail stick. Stick the heads in place with a little egg white or gum arabic. Leave the figures to dry for at least 12 hours, preferably on a sheet of foam.

3 Slice the top off the cake so it is completely flat.

4 Cut a 2.5 cm (1 inch) strip from each side of the cake. Cut a 7 cm (3 inch) strip

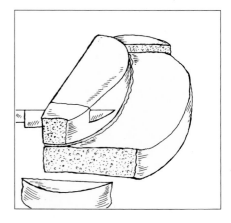

from the back. Spread the base of the 7 cm (3 inch) strip with half of the butter cream and place on top of the cake for the top stage. Trim 2.5 cm (1 inch) from each side of the top stage to neaten the shape.

5 Spread a thin layer of butter cream all over the cake to help the fondant stick and to thoroughly seal the cake to prevent crumbs.

6 Roll out the white fondant icing and cover the entire cake, gently moulding the fondant around the shape with your hands. Then place the cake towards the back of the round cake board, leaving enough room for the covered 25 cm (10 inch) square cake board to stand upright, leaning against the back of the cake.

7 Roll out 100g (3½oz) of the white modelling fondant and cut 2 strips each measuring 2.5 cm (1 inch) wide, and long enough to cover both the front and the sides of the top and bottom stage.

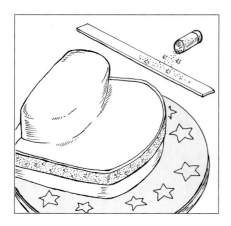

8 Thinly paint the surface of each strip with a little egg white or gum arabic, then sprinkle the white glitter all over. Lift the strips gently and stick in place on the front of each stage.

9 Cut 25g (1oz) of the white modelling fondant into 3 equal pieces and roll into balls. Cut each ball in half to make 6 spotlights. Set aside to dry.

10 When the strippers are dry, prop them up on their feet leaning against something solid, but with easy access to their heads. Using the No. 3 piping nozzle and the cream royal icing, pipe the hair on 2 of the strippers. Make the hair quite long at the back, as when the royal icing dries, it holds the head firmly in place. Pipe the hair on 3 more strippers, making 1 a redhead and 2 with brown hair, once again using the No. 3 piping nozzle.

11 With half of the black royal icing, pipe a slight bulge in the front of 4 of the strippers (or bigger if you wish!), using the No. 3 piping nozzle. With the remaining black royal icing and the No. 1 piping nozzle, pipe the lines for the strippers' G-strings. Pipe the dark brown stripper's curly black hair. Leave the icing to dry.

12 Mix the silver lustre powder with the clear alcohol and paint the stars on both of the cake boards with a fine paintbrush. Paint a little silver on the front of each spotlight.

13 With the white royal icing and the No. 2 piping nozzle, stick the silver ribbon in place. Stick the square board to the back of the cake. Pipe the wing collars. Stick the strippers in position with a little royal icing piped on the bottom of each foot and a little on their behinds. Stick the spotlights in place, with 2 on the top stage and 4 on the bottom stage.

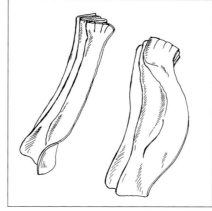

14 Roll out 200g (7oz) of the white modelling fondant and cut an oblong measuring 25 x 15 cm (10 x 6 inches) for one of the curtains. Fold the top 4 times to pleat. Indent with a cocktail stick. Stick on to the square board with royal icing and let it drape naturally. Repeat for the other curtain. With the modelling fondant trimmings, cut out 3 scarves and stick in place around 3 of the strippers.

15 With the red royal icing and the No. 2 piping nozzle, pipe the strippers' bow ties in place.

16 Leave the cake to dry for at least 8 hours, or overnight to allow the icing to dry thoroughly.

17 With the black food colouring pen, carefully draw the eyes and eyebrows to give the strippers their cheeky expressions.

Alternative designs:

For an added touch of fun, you could make a microphone using modelling fondant trimmings. You would need only a tiny amount to shape a portable microphone, a tiny ball for the top and a small sausage shape for the base. For the piece of wire, roll the icing into a thin sausage shape and stick it on to the base of the microphone using a little egg white or gum arabic. Finally, you could paint the top of the microphone with a little of the silver lustre paste. Instead of silver stars on the cake board, why not paint them gold, using gold lustre powder, see page 23 for instructions.

Bathtime Fun

A cheeky cake for an anniversary celebration perhaps — they that bath together, stay together?

You will need:

1 Madeira cake (size 1)
1.075kg (2lb 6oz) fondant icing
325g (11½oz) modelling fondant
250g (9oz) royal icing
blue, flesh, pink, yellow and brown food colouring paste
275g (10oz) butter cream
egg white or gum arabic
gold colour (see page 23)
black, pink and blue food colouring pens
clear piping gel

Equipment:

7–8 cocktail sticks
30 cm (12 inch) oval cake board
crimping tool
fine paintbrush
No. 3 piping nozzle
small blossom cutter

Colour:

Fondant icing: 300g (11oz) blue, 750g (1lb 11oz) white
Modelling fondant: 50g (2oz) white, 200g (7oz) flesh, 50g (2oz) pink, 10g (½oz) yellow
Royal icing: 175g (6oz) blue, 50g (2oz) brown, 25g (1oz) white

1 Cover the cake board with the blue fondant. Make small even cuts with a sharp knife all round the edge for the carpet fringe. Gently push the crimping tool into the icing and crimp a line following the fringe. Leave to dry.

2 Slice the top off the cake so it is completely flat.

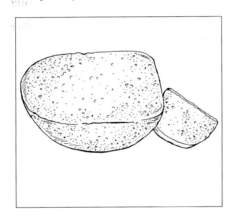

3 To make the base of the bath more rounded, trim the edge at the bottom of the cake. Trim one end straight for the taps.

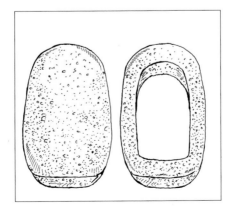

4 Cut a layer in the cake 2.5 cm (1 inch) from the top. Cut out the centre of this layer, so you have an oval-shaped rim about 2 cm (¾ inch) wide.

5 Spread 150g (5oz) of the butter cream on the top of the cake, then replace the rim.

6 Turn the cake upside down and spread butter cream thinly all over the base and sides to help the fondant stick.

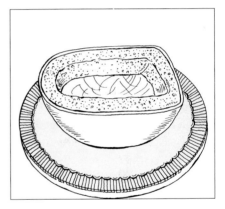

7 Roll out 450g (1lb) of the white fondant icing and cover the cake completely, then trim around the rim. Carefully lift the cake and place on the cake board right side up.

8 Cover the rim of the cake with a thin layer of butter cream. Roll out the remaining white fondant icing and place over the top of the bath. Smooth over the rim, letting it overlap slightly, then trim.

9 Cut 20g (¾oz) of the white modelling fondant into 4 equal pieces and model the bath legs, marking the lines with a cocktail stick. Use a little egg white or gum arabic to stick in place.

35

10 Take 10g (½ oz) of the white modelling fondant and cut in half to make the 2 taps. Each tap is made by rolling 3 small balls, one of which is flattened slightly. Cut out 4 triangles from the flattened ball to make the top of the tap. Roll a small sausage shape and bend at one end. Assemble the taps by placing one ball on the bath, followed by the sausage shape, another ball and the top, sticking them in place with a little egg white or gum arabic. Indent the top of the tap with the tip of the No. 3 nozzle.

11 With the remaining white modelling fondant, cut out a towel and a flannel, then fold. Model a small plug. Set aside to dry.

12 To make the woman, roll a ball with 65g (2½ oz) of the flesh-coloured modelling fondant, flatten slightly and cut the arms at the sides. Model the body shape. Cut a 5g (¼ oz) piece in half and model the boobs. Stick in place with the arms covering the boobs, using a little egg white or gum arabic. Roll a ball with 20g (¾ oz) for her head and a tiny ball for her nose, then indent the mouth using the tip of the No. 3 piping nozzle. Position in the bath with the back of her head resting on the rim, and stick in place.

13 To make the man, roll a ball with 65g (2½ oz) of the flesh-coloured modelling fondant, flatten slightly and cut the arms at the sides. Model the body shape and mark the chest with a cocktail stick. Position in the bath with one arm resting on the rim and the other with the hand stuck to the bath just under the tap. Roll a ball with 20g (¾ oz) for the head and roll a tiny ball for the nose. Mark the grin with a cocktail stick. Model the man's legs with 10g (½ oz) each. Put the legs in position and stick the head in place with a little egg white or gum arabic.

14 Spoon the blue royal icing into the bath and swirl round the bodies using a cocktail stick. Put a drip on the side of the bath.

15 With the pink modelling fondant, cut out a bath mat and make a row of small cuts in each end with a knife. Crimp a line above the cuts. Indent the flower pattern with the small blossom cutter. Cut out a towel and fold it up. With the trimmings, model the bar of soap. Stick the mat and towel to the board; and place the soap on the flannel made earlier, at the corner of the bath, using a little egg white or gum arabic.

16 With the blue fondant trimmings, cut out a towel and fold. Stick on top of the pink towel, then stick the white towel in place.

17 Cut the yellow modelling fondant in half and model the 2 ducks. Stick in place, one on the board and the other in the bath.

18 With the No. 3 piping nozzle and the brown royal icing, pipe the hair. 'Curl' with a cocktail stick.

19 With the same nozzle and the white royal icing, pipe the plug chain. Stick the plug to the man's hand.

20 Leave the cake to dry for at least 8 hours, or overnight.

21 Apply the gold colour to the bath feet, the plug and chain and the taps.

22 Draw the eyes and eyebrows with the black food colouring pen. With the pink and blue food colouring pens, draw the pattern on the side of the bath.

23 Using a fine paintbrush, paint a little clear piping gel on to the royal icing in the bath to make the water look wet.

Right: Bathtime fun

Motor Show

*Two of a fella's favourite things in life — but which one does he like best,
the blonde bombshell or the sports car?*

YOU WILL NEED:
1 Madeira cake (size 3)
1.075kg (2lb 6oz) fondant icing
375g (13oz) modelling fondant
25g (1oz) royal icing
red, black, flesh and egg yellow
   food colouring paste
silver lustre powder
2 tablespoons clear alcohol, eg
   vodka or gin
450g (1lb) butter cream
egg white or gum arabic
1 tablespoon confectioners glaze
black and blue food colouring pens
red dusting powder

EQUIPMENT:
5–6 cocktail sticks
35 cm (14 inch) hexagonal cake
   board
large, medium and fine paintbrush
5 cm (2 inch) and 2.5 cm (1 inch)
   plain circle cutters
No. 4 piping nozzle
foam

COLOUR:
Fondant icing: 475g (1lb 1oz) white,
   475g (1lb 1oz) red, 125g (4oz)
   black
Modelling fondant: 150g (5oz) grey,
   150g (5oz) black, 65g (2½oz)
   flesh, 10g (½oz) white
Royal icing: 25g (1oz) cream (a
   touch of egg yellow)

1 Cover the cake board with the white fondant. When the fondant is dry, mix the silver lustre powder with the clear alcohol and paint over the surface. Paint 2 coats to cover completely, letting the silver colour dry between coats. Reserve the remaining silver paste.

2 Slice the top off the cake so it is completely flat.

3 Cut a strip lengthways measuring 12 cm (5 inches) wide for the base of the car. Now cut a layer in the remaining 7 cm (3 inch) strip and place the two pieces on top of the car base and trim.

4 Measure 15 cm (6 inches) from the front of the car and trim out a seat measuring 9 cm (3½ inches) across and 5 cm (2 inches) in length, cutting down to the top of the second layer. Cut a slight curve for the windscreen.

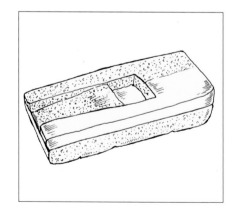

5 For the bonnet, make a cut on each side about 1 cm (½ inch) from the side of the cake, cutting at a slight angle up towards the windscreen. Trim the centre of the bonnet so it slopes downwards.

6 To shape the boot, make a straight cut on either side about 1 cm (½ inch) from the side of the cake. Trim out the centre of the boot, sloping downwards.

7 Trim the cake to round off any angles. Trim a little from round the base of the cake for the fondant to tuck under.

8 Sandwich the 2 layers together with half of the butter cream.

9 To mark an outline for the 4 wheels, carefully push the 5 cm (2 inch) circle cutter into the cake by about 5 mm (¼ inch). Trim out a little cake to make room for the wheels.

10 Spread a thin layer of butter cream all over the cake to help the fondant stick and prevent crumbs.

11 Roll out the red fondant into an oblong, lift carefully and cover the entire cake. Smooth into shape, pushing the icing gently into the seat. Trim round the base, tucking the fondant underneath.

12 Using a knife, mark the lines for the bonnet, the boot and the 2 doors. Cut out the marked wheel areas, smoothing the fondant round the curves. Place the cake on the fondant-covered cake board.

13 Roll out half of the black fondant icing and cut out 4 circles using the 5 cm (2 inch) circle cutter. Cover the wheel areas.

14 Roll out the remaining black fondant and cut an oblong for the seat, measuring 7 x 8 cm (3 x 3½ inches). Mark the lines with a knife and place on the cake. Roll the trimmings into a sausage shape, tapering at the ends, for the rolled-up roof. Stick in place with a little egg white or gum arabic.

15 Cut a 40g (1½oz) piece of the grey modelling fondant in half, roll 2 sausage shapes, flatten slightly, and stick on the car for the front and back bumpers.

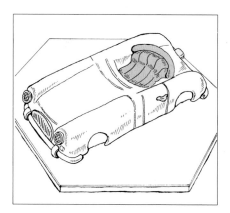

16 Cut a 5g (¼oz) piece of the grey fondant in half and model the 2 headlights. Push the end of a piping nozzle into each headlight to indent a circle, then mark the criss-cross pattern with a knife. With another 20g (¾oz), model the 2 door handles, key locks, the boot handle and 4 small hooks, 2 for each bumper. Roll out 25g (1oz) and cut a grille for the front of the car. Indent the lines with a knife. Model 2 side lights from the trimmings. Stick everything in place with a little egg white or gum arabic.

17 To make the windscreen, roll out the remaining grey modelling fondant and cut an oblong measuring 4 x 10 cm (1½ x 4 inches). Mark the lines round the edge with a knife. Shape into a slight curve and set aside for about 10 minutes to harden. Trim out a little red fondant to make a slot for the windscreen. Paint egg white or gum arabic on to the base of the windscreen and slot in place on top of the car. Model the 2 windscreen wipers from the trimmings and set aside to dry.

18 Mix a little of the black food colouring paste with a few drops of water or clear alcohol and paint a thin coat on the front of the windscreen using the fine paintbrush. Stick the windscreen wipers in place.

19 To make the wheels, divide 125g (4oz) of the black modelling fondant into 4 equal pieces. Roll 4 balls, then flatten slightly. Indent the centre of each with the 2.5 cm (1 inch) circle cutter, then mark the lines for the wire wheels with a knife. Roll 4 tiny balls for the centre of each wheel and stick them in place.

20 Model the girl's costume with the remaining black modelling fondant.

21 With 15g (½ oz) of the flesh-coloured modelling fondant, roll a ball for the girl's head. Mark the smile with a cocktail stick and roll a tiny ball for her nose. Divide the remaining fondant into 3 equal pieces. Roll sausage shapes and model her 2 legs and the top of her body with her arms. Stick together with the black costume using a little egg white or gum arabic and arrange in her pose on the bonnet of the car, then stick her head on top. Use a piece of foam for support while drying, if needed.

22 With the reserved silver lustre paste and a fine paintbrush, paint the grille, bumpers, lights, handles, key locks, 4 wheel centres, the wipers and the surround on the windscreen.

23 With the white modelling fondant, make 2 tiny eyes and the sash and stick in place.

24 Pipe the girl's hair with the cream-coloured royal icing and the No. 4 piping nozzle.

25 With the medium paintbrush, paint 1-2 layers of confectioners glaze over the car and the girl's costume, then leave the cake to dry for at least 8 hours, or overnight.

26 Draw the eyes and eyebrows with the black food colouring pen and colour the eyes with the blue pen. Dust a little of the red dusting powder on to her cheeks and lips.

Riding the Waves

This naughty cake would certainly make waves at an engagement or housewarming party.

YOU WILL NEED:
1 Madeira cake (size 10)
975g (2lb 3oz) fondant icing
800g (1lb 12oz) modelling fondant
175g (6oz) royal icing
red, black, flesh, egg yellow and
  blue food colouring paste
200g (7oz) butter cream
egg white or gum arabic
red and black food colouring pens
red dusting powder
2 tablespoons clear piping jelly

EQUIPMENT:
5-6 cocktail sticks
35 cm (14 inch) heart-shaped cake
  board
fine paintbrush
foam
No. 3 piping nozzle
greaseproof paper piping bag

COLOUR:
Fondant icing: 375g (13oz) red, 625g
  (1lb 6oz) white
Modelling fondant: 350g (12oz)
  white, 150g (5oz) black, 300g
  (11oz) flesh
Royal icing: 25g (1oz) black, 25g
  (1oz) cream (a touch of egg
  yellow), 125g (4oz) pale blue

1 Cover the cake board with the red fondant and leave to dry.

2 Slice the top off the cake where it has risen, leaving the sides rounded, and trim to neaten.

3 Carefully turn the cake over and trim away the edge so as to round off the cake sides.

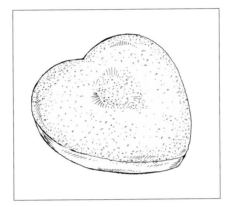

4 Turn the cake right side up and trim out the centre of the cake, cutting in at an angle to a depth of about 4 cm (1½ inches).

5 Spread a thin layer of butter cream all over the cake to help the fondant stick and prevent crumbs.

6 Roll out the white fondant and cover the cake completely. Tuck the icing under the base, then place the cake on the cake board. Mark the crease lines from the centre outwards with the end of a paintbrush. Make a cut in the side of the bed for the split.

7 Cut 150g (5oz) of the white modelling fondant in half and model 2 pillows. Position one falling on the floor on the man's side and the other on the bed.

8 Model 2 more pillows using the black modelling fondant. Tuck one under the white pillow and place the other on the other side of the bed.

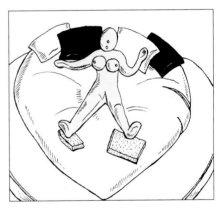

9 The man and woman are made with 125g (4oz) of the flesh-coloured modelling fondant for each body, 15g (½ oz) for each head and out of the remaining fondant the boobs, nipples and 2 tiny noses are modelled. To make the woman's body, roll a sausage shape and make a cut half way down for the legs. Flatten slightly and cut the arms away from the sides, then model the body shape. Stick the head and nose, boobs and nipples in position on the body with a little egg white or gum arabic. Use pieces of foam for support while drying. Position her on the bed first.

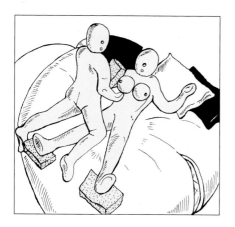

10 Model the man in the same way and position him on the bed with his right leg between the woman's, using his left arm to prop himself up. Again, use pieces of foam for support while drying. Indent the open mouths using the tip of the piping nozzle.

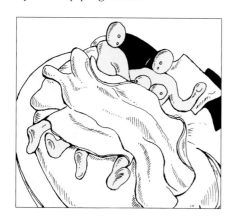

11 Roll out the remaining white modelling fondant and cut out a neat oblong measuring 20 x 25 cm (8 x 10 inches) for the bedcover. Drape it over the bed, covering up all the naughty bits and encouraging folds to look like rumpled bedclothes.

12 With the black royal icing and the No. 3 piping nozzle, carefully pipe the woman's long hair.

13 With the cream-coloured royal icing and the No. 3 piping nozzle, carefully pipe the man's hair.

14 Put the pale blue royal icing into a greaseproof paper piping bag and snip off the end to make a fairly large hole.

Squeeze the icing out below the split in the bed, letting it fall downwards and on to the fondant-covered board. Pipe water droplets on the bedcover and nearest pillow.

15 Leave the cake to dry for at least 8 hours, or overnight.

16 With the red food colouring pen, draw the little decorative hearts all over the bed. Draw the eyes and eyebrows on the two faces with the black food colouring pen.

17 Mix a little of the black food colouring paste with a few drops of water. Using a fine paintbrush, paint the zebra stripes on the bedcover.

18 Dust both of the figures' cheeks and the woman's boobs with a little of the red dusting powder.

19 Place the clear piping jelly into a greaseproof paper piping bag with the end snipped off and pipe over the pale blue royal icing to make it look more like water.

Right: Riding the waves

Alternative design:

To create an even raunchier look, paint a leopard print on to the bedclothes. Water down a little orange, brown and black food colouring paste with a few drops of water or clear alcohol. Using a fine paintbrush, paint the leopard print design on to bedclothes that have been coloured pale yellow.

Over Exposed!

A birthday or retirement cake for a dirty old man — but tell him to keep his trousers on under the raincoat!

YOU WILL NEED:

5 Madeira cakes (size 5, size 6, size 7, size 8)

1.925kg (4lb 4oz) fondant icing

blue, flesh, brown, black and red food colouring paste

575g (1lb 4oz) butter cream

egg white or gum arabic

black, red and blue food colouring pens

EQUIPMENT:

7-8 cocktail sticks

25 cm (10 inch) round cake board

fine paintbrush

10 cm (4 inch) plain circle cutter

skewer or dowelling

COLOUR:

Fondant icing: 250g (9oz) blue, 375g (13oz) flesh, 700g (1lb 9oz) light brown, 225g (8oz) grey, 275g (10oz) dark brown, 75g (3oz) red, 5g ($^1/_4$oz) white

1 Cover the cake board with the blue fondant and leave to dry. Reserve the trimmings for the eyes.

2 Slice the tops off all the cakes so they are completely flat.

3 Slice a layer in the 15 cm (6 inch) round cake and place the 12 cm (5 inch) round cake in between, towards the back. Place the large bowl cake on top.

4 To mark the arms, make a cut about 1 cm ($^1/_2$ inch) deep near the top of the bowl cake, and continue in a curving line down to the bottom of the bowl cake. Mark the back of the arm curving similarly 5 cm (2 inches) behind the first line. Repeat for the other arm.

5 Slice down the front, keeping the tummy area a little rounded, and trim round to the arms. Slice downwards at the back, keeping the bottom area rounded, again trim round to the arms.

6 Slice out a piece of cake directly underneath each arm. Trim the base of the cake to make the feet and trim out

a thin wedge at the front and back to mark the legs. Trim the edges off the arms and trim any angles that are left round the cake.

7 Sandwich the 3 layers together with half of the butter cream and place the cake in the centre of the cake board.

8 Sandwich the 2 small bowl cakes together with butter cream to make the head. Trim the front almost flat to shape the face. Set aside.

9 Spread a thin layer of butter cream over the surface of the head and body cakes to help the fondant stick.

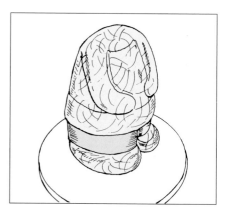

10 Roll out 150g (5oz) of the flesh-coloured fondant and cut a strip measuring at least 4 x 38 cm (1$^1/_2$ x 15 inches). Wrap round the legs, making the join at the back.

11 With another 50g (2oz), roll a quarter into a ball for the hidden hand and use the rest to model the hand that shows. Mark the fingers with a cocktail stick and set aside.

12 Make the 2 ears out of a 15g (1/2oz) piece of flesh-coloured fondant and set aside. Divide another 15g (1/2oz) into 6 pieces and use to pad out the face: roll 3 tiny balls, 2 for the cheeks and 1 for the chin, and 3 tiny sausage shapes, 2 for the eyebrows and 1 for the bottom lip. With another 15g (1/2oz), model the nose. Position on the face, then roll out the remaining fondant and cover the face, smoothing out the features with your fingers. Mark the eyes and grin with a cocktail stick.

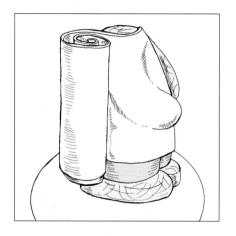

13 To make the flasher's mac, roll out 575g (1lb 4oz) of the light brown fondant icing and cut out a neat oblong measuring 15 x 50 cm (6 x 20 inches). Carefully roll up the fondant to make it easier to handle, place one short edge against the front for the opening, then gradually unroll the fondant all the way round the cake. Trim at the join, letting the mac overlap slightly. Gently mould the fondant round the flasher's arms and mark the creases carefully with a cocktail stick.

14 Push the 'hidden hand' made in step 11 into the mac opening and stick in place with a little egg white or gum arabic. Stick on the hand holding a little of the mac open.

15 With the light brown fondant trimmings, cut out the collar and the 2 cuffs. Stick in place and mark the button holes and stitching detail with the tip of a knife.

16 To make the cap, roll out the remaining light brown fondant about 1 cm (1/2 inch) thick. Indent the peak with the skewer and roll the front slightly thinner. Cut out the cap with the 10 cm (4 inch) circle cutter and set aside.

17 Put the head on the cake and push the skewer or dowelling down through the top of the head to keep in place.

18 Roll out the grey fondant thickly and cover the top and back of the head. Pinch to 'curl' the hair and pinch down the sideburns. Stick the ears in place and stick the cap on top of his head at a slight angle.

19 Pad out the front of each shoe with a 25g (1oz) piece of the dark brown fondant. Roll out the remaining fondant, cut in half and cover each shoe completely. Indent the top of the shoes with the circle cutter.

20 To make the scarf, roll out the red fondant and cut a strip at least 30 cm (12 inches) long. Make small cuts in each end to fringe. Wrap round the flasher's neck and fold over the front. With the red fondant trimmings, model the tongue and stick in place with a little egg white or gum arabic.

21 Take a small piece of the white fondant and model one eye. With a tiny amount of the blue trimmings, make the iris. Stick in place with a little egg white or gum arabic. Leave the cake for at least 8 hours, or overnight to

allow the icing to dry thoroughly.

22 Draw the eyebrows, eyes and eyelashes and the hairy legs with the black food colouring pen. With the red and blue food colouring pens, draw the tartan design on his cap.

Maid Service!

As a birthday treat, you could offer maid service for the day — little black dress optional!

You will need:

1 quick mix cake (size 4)
925g (2lb 1oz) fondant icing
225g (8oz) modelling fondant
125g (4oz) royal icing
green, peach, orange, brown, flesh
  and black food colouring paste
350g (12oz) butter cream
egg white or gum arabic
black, peach and green food
  colouring pens
silver lustre powder

Equipment:

9-10 cocktail sticks
30 cm (12 inch) petal-shaped cake
  board
crimping tool
leaf embossing stamp
7 cm (3 inch) and 4 cm (1½ inch)
  plain circle cutters
round-headed pin
garrett frill cutter
fine paintbrush
foam
No. 2 and No. 3 piping nozzles
small piece of white voile net (tulle)

Colour:

Fondant icing: 275g (10oz) pale
  green, 500g (1lb 2oz) peach, 150g
  (5oz) orange-brown
Modelling fondant: 100g (3½oz)
  flesh, 100g (3½oz) black, 25g
  (1oz) white
Royal icing: 25g (1oz) white, 40g
  (1½oz) black, 40g (1½oz) green

1 Cover the cake board completely using the pale green fondant, reserving all the trimmings.

2 Crimp all round the edge and press the leaf embossing stamp gently into the icing for the carpet pattern. Set aside and leave to dry.

3 Slice the top off the cake so it is completely flat.

4 Cut a strip from the cake measuring 8 x 20 cm (3½ x 8 inches) to make the the chaise longue. Out of the remaining cake, cut 2 circles with the 7 cm (3 inch) circle cutter, cut an oblong measuring 4 x 8 cm (1½ x 3½ inches) for the top of the chaise longue, and another one measuring 1 x 7 cm (½ x 3 inches) for the armrest.

5 Slice a layer in one of the round cakes and put one layer on top of the other round cake, then cut 2 small circles out of the second layer using the 4 cm (1½ inch) circle cutter. Then assemble the chaise longue together as shown in the illustration. Trim the

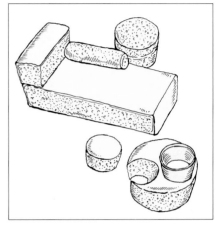

chaise longue to round off the edges and trim one side of the headrest into a curve.

6 Sandwich the 2 layers of the table together with a little butter cream and stick the head and armrest on to the chaise longue.

7 Spread a thin layer of butter cream over all the cakes to help the fondant stick and to seal the cakes to prevent crumbs.

8 Roll out 375g (13oz) of the peach fondant and cover the chaise longue completely, smoothing into shape with your hands. Mark the lines and creases with a knife.

9 Roll out the remaining peach-coloured fondant and cut out a circle 20 cm (8 inches) in diameter. Place the fondant over the table cake, encouraging the pleats. Position the table on the cake board with the chaise longue in front of it at a slight angle.

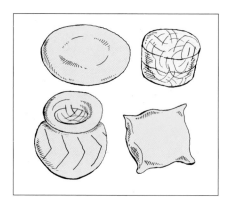

10 To make the terracotta plant pots, roll a 50g (2oz) ball with the orange-brown fondant, push your thumb in the centre and mould round to make a well for one of the small circle cakes to sit in. Push the fondant up and over the cake, then pinch round the top for the rim. Mark the pattern with a knife. Repeat for the second plant pot. Make a cushion with some of the remaining orange-brown fondant.

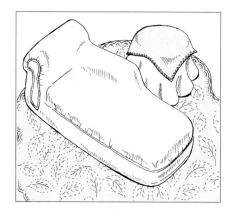

11 With the pale green fondant trimmings, model a cushion and roll out and cut a square for the table cover. Indent the edge of the cover with the end of a round-headed pin, then drape over the table.

12 Using some of the peach fondant trimmings, colour a 25g (1oz) piece a slightly deeper peach shade and model another cushion. Place the 3 cushions at one end of the chaise longue.

13 With the remaining peach fondant trimmings, make 2-3 garrett frills and stick them in position on the base of the chaise longue as soon as you have made them, using a little egg white or gum arabic.

14 To make the maid, start with her legs: roll a 75g (3oz) piece of the flesh-coloured modelling fondant into a sausage shape, then make a cut down the centre, starting 1 cm (½ inch) from the top. Model the legs and indent the bottom with a cocktail stick. Stick the legs to the side of the table with a little egg white or gum arabic and bend the bottom over slightly. Roll a ball for her head with a 15g (½ oz) piece and mark the mouth with the tip of the No. 3 piping nozzle. With the trimmings, make the 2 hands and a tiny nose. Set aside to dry.

15 Roll a 50g (2oz) piece of the black modelling fondant into a ball, flatten slightly and cut the arms away from the sides. Model the top of the body. Roll out the remaining black fondant and cut a circle for the skirt using the 7 cm (3 inch) circle cutter, model 2 small pieces to cover the insides of the plant pots, model 2 thin cone shapes for the base of the leaves and cut 2 thin strips for the stocking tops. Stick everything in place and use pieces of foam for support while drying, if needed.

16 With the white modelling fondant, make the 3 vases, 5 photo frames and the maid's bow and cap. Cut a small triangle for her knickers and stick in place. Model the top of the feather duster and mark the lines with a knife. Dampen the end of a cocktail stick with a little egg white or gum arabic, and push it into the 'feathers'. Lay flat and leave to dry.

17 With the white royal icing and the No. 2 piping nozzle, pipe the dots on the vase and the photo frames, and around her neckline and knickers. Cut the voile net into small pieces and position under her skirt, using the royal icing to secure.

18 With the black royal icing and the No. 3 piping nozzle, pipe the maid's hair. Position her cap on top of her head.

19 With the green royal icing and a piping bag with a 'V' cut in the tip, pipe the leaves on to the cone-shaped leaf bases in the plant pots.

20 Leave the cake to dry for at least 8 hours, or overnight.

21 With the black food colouring pen, draw the outlines on the photographs, eyes and eyebrows, and the stocking seams. Draw the pattern on the chaise longue and tablecloth using the peach and green food colouring pens.

22 Mix the silver lustre powder into a paste with a few drops of water. Paint a little on to the photo frames and the vase. Push the feather duster into the top of the table at an angle so the cocktail stick rests against the maid's hand.

Right: Maid service!

Can Can Girl

For any celebration, this sensationally frilly cake will go down well with a bottoms up toast!

You will need:

1 light fruit cake (size 2)
750g (1lb 11oz) fondant icing
275g (10oz) modelling fondant
25g (1oz) royal icing
pink, black and flesh food colouring paste
3 tablespoons apricot glaze or lemon curd
egg white or gum arabic
silver lustre powder
1 teaspoon clear alcohol

Equipment:

pastry brush
25 cm (10 inch) round cake board
3–4 cocktail sticks
fine paintbrush
garrett frill cutter
2.5 cm (1 inch) plain circle cutter
No. 1 piping nozzle

Colour:

Fondant icing: 625g (1lb 6oz) bright pink, 75g (3oz) mid pink, 50g (2oz) light pink
Modelling fondant: 175g (6oz) black, 125g (4oz) flesh
Royal icing: 25g (1oz) black

1 Trim the top off the cake, turn it upside down and place on the cake board. Brush the cake with apricot glaze or lemon curd to help the fondant stick.

2 Roll out the bright pink fondant and cover the cake completely. Trim round the base of the cake.

3 Roll out the black modelling fondant and cut a strip measuring 4 x 65 cm (1½ x 26 inches). Run the end of the paintbrush along one long edge to stretch and frill. Using a little egg white or gum arabic, stick the frill around the edge of the cake, letting it overlap very slightly.

4 With the bright pink fondant trimmings, make 5 garrett frills for the first layer, using the 2.5 cm (1 inch) circle cutter for the centres. Make the second layer with 4 garrett frills. Stick each frill in place as soon as it is made, using the black frill on the outer edge as a guide.

5 For the third and fourth layers, make 6–7 garrett frills using the mid-pink coloured fondant.

6 Make 5 garrett frills with the light pink fondant for the following 2 layers, saving the trimmings to make the final layer later.

7 To make the dancer's legs, roll a sausage shape with the flesh-coloured modelling fondant and make a cut

down the centre, starting 2.5 cm (1 inch) from the top. Model the legs and feet, then carefully place on the cake, letting the dancer's legs push the garrett frills down.

8 With the black modelling fondant trimmings, make the dancer's knickers and 2 small strips for the garters. Stick in place, then use the bright pink fondant trimmings to model the 2 tiny roses and cut a thin strip for the centre of each garter.

9 With the remaining pale pink fondant, make a garrett frill and arrange the final layer round the dancer's bottom. Cut out a small piece for between the legs.

10 With the black royal icing and the No. 1 piping nozzle, pipe the stocking seams down the centre of each leg, then pipe small dots round the edge of the knickers and the garters.

11 Mix the silver lustre powder and the clear alcohol into a paste and paint the stripes on the black frill with a fine paintbrush.

12 Leave the cake to dry for at least 8 hours, or overnight.

Alternative designs:

Although pink is the classic colour, you could always make the frills and 2 tiny roses a pretty pale yellow or soft peach instead.

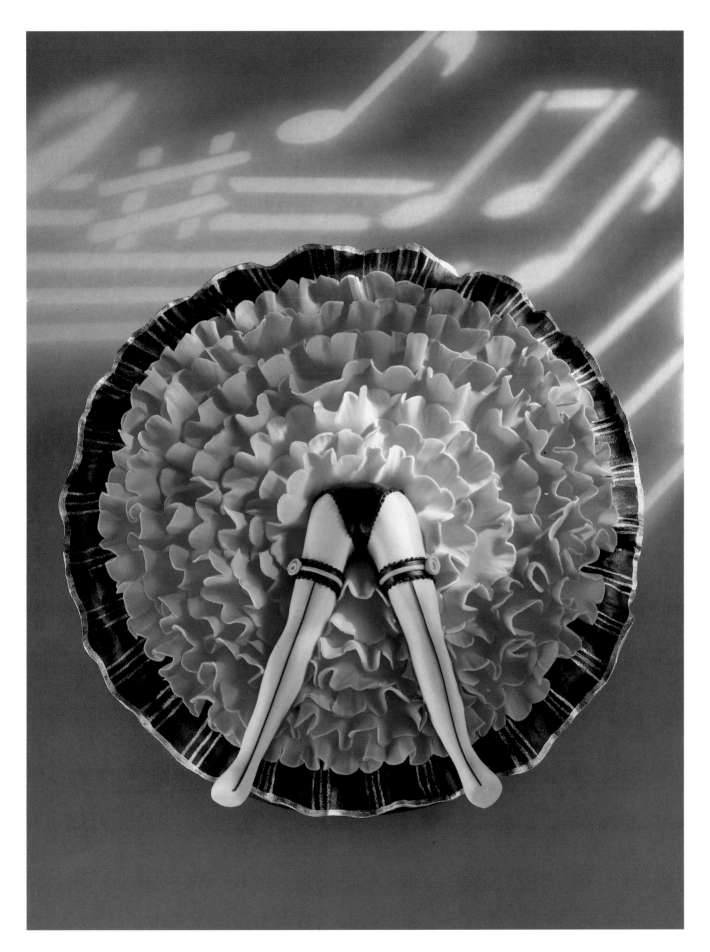

Strip Poker!

Getting caught without your underpants can be very embarrassing,
so ensure you're among friends when you deal this winner.

1 Cover the cake board with the green, grey and white streaky fondant. Using the crimping tool, crimp a line all round the edge of the board. Leave to dry.

2 Slice the top off the cake so it is completely flat.

3 Cut a 5 cm (2 inch) strip from the back of the cake, then cut the strip into 4 equal size pieces for the chair bases.

4 Cut a 5 cm (2 inch) strip from the short side of the cake, to leave a 15 cm (6 inch) square cake for the table.

5 To give a little more height, slice a layer in the table cake and sandwich back together with 200g (7oz) of the butter cream. Spread a thin layer of butter cream over the surface of each cake to help the fondant stick and to seal the cake to prevent crumbs. Reserve a little butter cream to stick the chair backs on later. Place the table cake on the centre of the cake board with the corners pointing to a straight edge.

6 To make the tablecloth, roll out 425g (15oz) of the white fondant icing and cut a square measuring 25 x 25 cm

(10 x 10 inches). Trim the corners to round off, then gently lift the tablecloth and place over the table, encouraging the pleats to form.

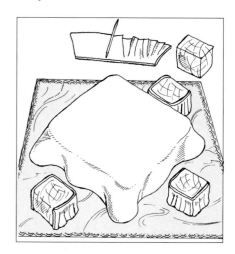

7 To make the frills for the 4 chairs, roll out 75g (3oz) of the white fondant icing for each frill and cut a strip measuring 15 x 5 cm (6 x 2 inches). Roll the top of a cocktail stick along the bottom edge to stretch the fondant slightly, then press the cocktail stick into the icing to mark the pleats. Wrap round a chair, leaving the back uncovered. Gently rub the top to round off the edges. Repeat for the other 3 chairs and then position all the chairs around the table on the cake board.

8 Roll out the dark green fondant icing and cut out a neat square measuring 15 x 15 cm (6 x 6 inches). Drape this over the table-cloth at an angle. With the dark green fondant trimmings, cut out 4 seat cushions measuring 5 x 5 cm (2 x 2 inches) and place one on each of the chairs.

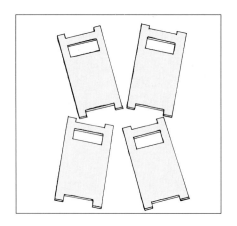

9 Roll out a quarter of the grey modelling fondant and cut out a chair back measuring 5 x 10 cm (2 x 4 inches). Trim a small piece from the top and bottom, then cut out an oblong from the chair back. Using the remaining grey fondant, make 3 more chair backs and set them all aside to dry, preferably on a sheet of foam.

10 To make the lampshade, roll a 50g (2oz) piece of the white modelling fondant into a ball, then pinch round the top 5 times. Shape the base and pinch gently all the way round. Mark the lines with a knife. Gently push the skewer or dowelling about 1 cm (¹/₂ inch) into the underside to make a hole for assembling the lamp later. Remove the skewer, then leave the lampshade to dry.

11 Roll out a 15g (¹/₂ oz) piece of the white modelling fondant and cut 2 circles, one 4 cm (1¹/₂ inches) and the other 2.5 cm (1 inch) in diameter. Stick these in position on the centre of the table using a little egg white or gum arabic. Before the icing dries, make a hole for the skewer or dowelling by pushing it gently down through the centre of the 2 circles, then remove.

12 Roll out 20g (³/₄oz) of the white modelling fondant and cut 24 or more tiny cards. With the trimmings, cut out 9 tiny bows and screw up 2 small pieces for the socks. Set aside to dry.

Right: Detail of the laughing lady

13 With a 40g (1¹/₂oz) piece, model the boxer shorts for the man holding the cards and stick in place on the chair using a little egg white or gum arabic.

14 Using three-quarters of the mauve modelling fondant, model the modest lady's skirt and stick in place on the chair using a little egg white or gum arabic. Roll out the remaining mauve fondant and cut a square, then fold it and stick in place on the floor at the front of the cake.

15 Using 50g (2oz) of the yellow modelling fondant, roll a ball and flatten slightly. Cut the 2 arms and model the modest lady's top. Hollow the underneath slightly with your thumb so the top fits neatly over the mauve skirt. Stick in place with the arms up. Roll out the remaining yellow fondant and cut a square, then gather it up to pleat and stick in place over a chair back.

16 Roll the grey-blue modelling fondant into a sausage shape, flatten slightly and make a cut along three-quarters of the length. Model the trousers and

hollow out the top, make a cut in the front for the open zip. Leave to dry.

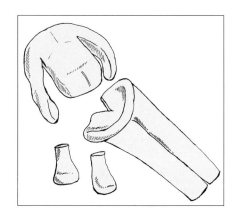

17 To make the man who's showing his bare bottom, roll a 75g (3oz) piece of the flesh-coloured modelling fondant into a ball, flatten slightly and cut the 2 arms. Shape the body and mark the bottom with a cocktail stick. Model the 2 feet. With a little egg white or gum arabic, stick the trousers made earlier to the side of the table, with the feet at the bottom, then push the chair right up against the legs to hold them steady. Stick the body in place with the hands holding the zip. If needed, use pieces of foam to support while drying.

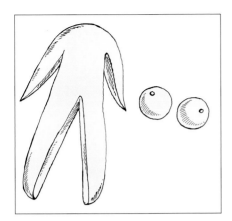

18 To make the laughing lady, roll 100g (3¹/₂oz) of the flesh-coloured modelling fondant into a sausage shape and flatten slightly. Make a cut for the legs about half way up and cut the 2 arms. Shape the body and stick in place with a little egg white or gum arabic. Support the arm with a piece of foam while drying. Roll 2 5g (¹/₄oz) balls for the boobs and stick on the body. Model 2 tiny balls for the nipples and stick them on the boobs.

19 For the man holding the cards, model the body as before, using a 50g (2oz) piece of the flesh-coloured modelling fondant. Mark the chest with a cocktail stick and stick in place on the white boxer shorts.

20 Roll 4 heads with 20g (³/₄oz) each and model 4 tiny noses. Mark the smiles with a cocktail stick, and stick all the heads in place with a little egg white or gum arabic.

21 With the remaining flesh-coloured modelling fondant, model 2 small hands for the modest lady and her 2 legs from below the knee. Make 2 legs for the man holding the cards and stick them in place.

22 Spread the remaining butter cream on the back of each chair base and press the chair backs in position.

23 Using the black modelling fondant, make the laughing lady's underwear

and the 2 shoes. Stick the socks made earlier on to the top of each shoe, then stick in place with a little egg white or gum arabic.

24 Roll out the red modelling fondant and cut out 2 squares. Drape one at the laughing lady's feet and the other over the back of the chair of the man holding the cards.

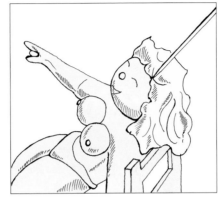

25 With the cream-coloured royal icing and the large plain piping nozzle, pipe the laughing lady's long hair and the hair for the man holding the playing cards. 'Curl' their hair with the end of a cocktail stick.

26 With the reddish brown-coloured royal icing pipe the modest lady's hair in place.

27 With the dark brown royal icing, pipe the hair for the man who is showing his bottom. Leave the cake for at least 8 hours, or overnight until the icing has dried thoroughly.

28 Using the food colouring pens, draw the playing cards, the floral design on the lampshade, the pretty tablecloth and chair pattern, the eyes and eyebrows on the figures, the bra straps on the floor and finally the red hearts on the boxer shorts.

29 With the white royal icing stick all the playing cards in place. Stick the bows on the sides of the chairs, and one on the lampshade. Carefully push

the skewer into the centre of the table. Dab a little royal icing on the top of the skewer, then gently push on the lampshade.

30 Apply a tiny amount of the red dusting powder to the laughing lady's cheeks and her boobs.

Alternative designs:

Depending on who the cake is for you could make this an all-male or indeed all-female gathering. Just model the figures accordingly and dress or undress them suitably! As for the clothing, if you have a particular item that would be perfect for the occasion, just model the clothes on your own! Finally, you could always change the pattern on the cloth — try making it a check cloth or match it to one you have at home.

Kama Sutra

If you take this book to bed with you for a good read, you'll end up with crumbs between the sheets!

You will need:

1 Victoria sponge cake (size 3) or
1 devil's food cake (size 1)
450g (1lb) fondant icing
750g (1lb 11oz) modelling fondant
egg yellow and brown food
colouring paste
150g (5oz) butter cream
egg white or gum arabic
1 tablespoon clear alcohol
gold (see page 23)

Equipment:

4–5 cocktail sticks
25 x 30 cm (10 x 12 inch) oblong
  cake board
rose-petal piping nozzle
greaseproof paper
piece of voile net
cake smoother
ruler
fine paintbrush
small piece of foam

Colour:

Fondant icing: 300g (11oz) cream (a
  touch of egg yellow), 150g (5oz)
  white
Modelling fondant: 750g (1lb 11oz)
  brown

KAMA
SUTRA

1 Cover the cake board with the cream fondant. To mark the 'stitching', gently push the tip of the rose-petal piping nozzle all round the edge of the fondant. Leave to dry.

2 Slice the top off the cake so it is completely flat. Cut a 4 cm (1½ inch) strip from one side of the cake so you are left with a book shape measuring 16 x 20 cm (6½ x 8 inches).

3 Spread a thin layer of butter cream all over the cake to help the fondant stick and prevent crumbs.

4 Trace the lettering on to a piece of greaseproof paper and set aside.

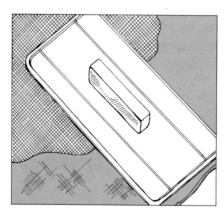

5 Roll out the brown modelling fondant and cut an oblong measuring 37 x 22 cm (15 x 8½ inches). Lay the piece of voile net on the icing and press the pattern into it using a cake smoother.

6 Carefully turn the icing over and lay half on the cake board. Put the cake in position, then wrap the icing over the top to make the book cover.

7 Using a long ruler, mark the crease for the book's binding. With the tip of the rose-petal piping nozzle, gently mark the 'stitching' all around the edge of the book cover.

8 Before the icing for the book cover dries, place the greaseproof paper with the lettering on it in position and carefully indent the outline of each letter into the surface of the icing using the tip of a cocktail stick.

9 Roll out the white fondant icing. Measure the 3 uncovered sides of the book cake and cut a strip of the white fondant to fit each one. Fix in place on the cake and mark the lines for the pages with a knife.

10 Using the brown modelling fondant trimmings, cut out the end of the bookmark. Stick in place with a little egg white or gum arabic.

11 To make the cover look more like leather, mix a little of the brown food colouring paste with the clear alcohol. Dip the small piece of foam into the colour, squeeze out the excess, then gently wipe the colour over the surface of the book cover and the bookmark. Use a paintbrush for any areas that prove difficult to reach.

12 Leave the cake to dry for at least 8 hours, or overnight.

13 Apply the gold colour to highlight the lettering and the 'stitching' round the edges.

A Pair of Boobs

Just watch everyone's eyes pop out when you carry this 'revealing' cake into the room!

You will need:

2 quick mix cakes (size 1) or 2 light fruit cakes (size 1)

1.475kg (3lb 4oz) fondant icing

flesh, black, red and brown food colouring paste

225g (8oz) butter cream (for the quick mix cakes) or 4 tablespoons apricot glaze or lemon curd (for the light fruit cakes)

egg white or gum arabic

1 silver dragee

Equipment:

5–6 cocktail sticks

30 cm (12 inch) heart-shaped cake board

pastry brush (for the apricot glaze)

4 cm (1½ inch) plain circle cutter

fine paintbrush

20 cm (8 inch) greaseproof paper circle

rose embossing stamp

garrett frill cutter

large blossom plunger cutter

Colour:

Fondant icing: 900g (2lb) flesh, 450g (1lb) black, 125g (4oz) red

1 Slice the tops off both cakes so they are completely flat. Set one of the tops to one side.

2 Place the reserved top in the centre of the cake board. This will help to give the boobs a better shape and added height when covered with icing.

If you are using quick mix cakes, spread 75g (3oz) of butter cream over the surface; if you have made light fruit cakes, brush the surface with 1 tablespoon of the apricot glaze or lemon curd.

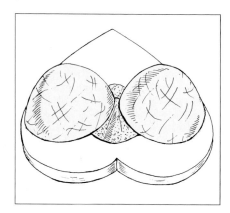

3 Place the 2 cakes directly on to the top of the board, at a slight angle, this makes the boobs look more natural. Spread a thin layer of butter cream or apricot glaze all over the cakes to help the fondant stick.

4 Dampen the cake board with a little water. Roll out the flesh-coloured fondant and lift carefully, by sliding your hands underneath. Place the fondant over both cakes and the cake board. Smooth the surface with your hands, pushing gently into the cleavage. Trim all round the edge of the cake board.

5 For the nipples, colour a little of the flesh fondant trimmings a reddish brown colour using a little of the red and brown food colouring paste. Roll out and cut 2 circles using the circle cutter. Stick in position slightly off centre (for a more natural look), using a little

egg white or gum arabic. Model 2 small balls and stick in position on the centre of each circle.

6 Roll out the black fondant. Using the greaseproof paper circle as a guide, cut out 2 20 cm (8 inch) circles. Cut away a half moon shape from the top of each circle, so that you are left with 2 bra cup shapes. Stick these in position on the boobs with a little egg white or gum arabic. Fold down the top right hand corner of the bra to expose the nipple, just a little!

7 Mark a design on the bra using the rose embossing stamp, gently pressing it into the icing.

8 Make garrett frills out of the black fondant trimmings. Stick on to the top of the bra cups using a little egg white or gum arabic. Cut 2 long thin pieces of black fondant for the bra straps and arrange on the cake board, sticking carefully in place.

9 Roll out the red fondant and cut 2 long thin strips. Stick in place on the edge of the garrett frill with a little egg white or gum arabic.

10 Using the blossom plunger cutter, make a little flower out of some of the red fondant trimmings. Place the silver dragee in the centre, then stick on the centre of the bra with a little egg white or gum arabic.

11 Leave the cake to dry for at least 8 hours, or overnight.

Cheeky Scotsman

Never ask a Scotsman what he's got under his kilt — he might decide to show you!

You will need:

5 Madeira cakes (size 5, size 6, size 7, size 8)

2.115kg (4lb 11½oz) fondant icing

green, flesh, black, orange and red food colouring paste

575g (1lb 4oz) butter cream

egg white or gum arabic

red, black and brown food colouring pens

red dusting powder

Equipment:

5–6 cocktail sticks

25 cm (10 inch) round cake board

skewer or dowelling

fine paintbrush

tartan ribbon

Colour:

Fondant icing: 600g (1lb 5oz) green, 625g (1lb 6oz) flesh, 50g (2oz) white, 600g (1lb 5oz) black, 225g (8oz) orange, 15g (½oz) red

1 Cover the cake board with 250g (9oz) of the green fondant and leave to dry.

2 Slice the tops off all the cakes so they are completely flat.

3 Slice a layer in the 15 cm (6 inch) round cake and place the 12 cm (5 inch) round cake in between, slightly towards the back. Place the large bowl cake on top.

4 To mark the arms, make a cut about 1 cm (½ inch) deep from the top of the bowl cake, cutting downwards and curving backwards. Stop at the top of the 12 cm (5 inch) cake. Mark the back of the arm with a similar curving line 5 cm (2 inches) behind the first line. Repeat for the other arm.

5 Slice down the front, keeping the tummy quite rounded, and trim round to the arms. Slice down the back, keeping the bottom area rounded, and trim round to the arms.

6 Slice out a piece of cake directly underneath each arm, then trim the base of the cake to make the Scotman's shoes. Trim out a thin wedge at the front and back of the cake to mark the legs, then trim off any angles that are left on the cake.

7 Sandwich together the 3 layers with half of the butter cream, then spread a thin layer of butter cream all over the cake to help the fondant stick and to seal the cake to prevent crumbs. Place in the centre of the cake board.

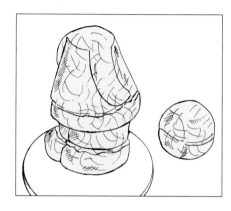

8 Sandwich the 2 small bowl cakes together with butter cream to make the head, and trim the front flat for the face. Spread a thin layer of butter cream all over the head and set aside.

9 Roll out 275g (10oz) of the flesh-coloured fondant and cut a strip measuring at least 5 x 40 cm (2 x 16 inches). Wrap round the legs and smooth over the join gently with your fingertips.

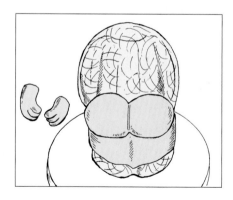

10 Divide 200g (7oz) of the flesh-coloured fondant into 4 equal pieces and roll into balls. Press 2 on to the cake for his bottom and model the other 2 into the hands. Mark the fingers with a cocktail stick and set aside to dry.

11 With 25g (1oz) of the flesh-coloured fondant, roll half into a ball for his nose. Divide the other half into 6 pieces and roll 3 small balls – 2 for his cheeks and 1 for the chin – and 3 very thin sausage shapes – 2 for his eyebrows and 1 for the bottom lip. Press in position on the face.

12 Roll out the remaining flesh-coloured fondant and cover the face, smoothing out the features. Mark the smiling eyes with a cocktail stick.

13 Roll out the white fondant and cover the top half of the front of the cake for the shirt. Position the head and push the skewer or dowelling down through the top to keep in place.

14 Roll out 150g (5oz) of the green fondant and cut a strip for the back of the kilt. Indent the pleats with a cocktail stick, pushing in only slightly or they may tear. Place on the cake, flicking up the hem. Stick the hands in place using a little egg white or gum arabic.

15 Roll out another 150g (5oz) and cut a strip for the front of the kilt. Again, mark the pleats with a cocktail stick, leaving a straight panel in the centre.

16 Roll a ball with the remaining green fondant, flatten slightly, and model the hat. Using the end of a paintbrush, indent 5 folds and smooth with your fingers. Set aside to dry.

17 To make the jacket, roll out 375g (13oz) of the black fondant and cut a strip measuring at least 10 x 40 cm (4 x 16 inches). Wrap round the cake with the join at the front. Roll over the top to make a collar. Smooth round the arms to shape. With the trimmings, model 3 buttons for the jacket and cut 2 cuffs. Stick in place with a little egg white or gum arabic.

18 Cut a 50g (2oz) piece of the black fondant in half and press on to the front of each shoe. Roll out the remaining black fondant, cut in half and cover each shoe completely.

19 With a 25g (1oz) piece of the orange fondant, model the beard and moustache and stick in place with a little egg white or gum arabic. Mark some lines on the moustache with a knife.

20 Roll out the remaining orange fondant about 1 cm (¹/₂ inch) thick and cover the top and back of the head. Pinch with your fingers to 'curl' the hair and pinch down the sideburns. Stick the hat in place on top of his head with egg white or gum arabic.

21 Roll a ball with the red fondant and stick on the top of the hat for the bobble. Fold the tartan ribbon in half and push the centre under the back of the hat, using a cocktail stick.

22 Leave the cake to dry for at least 8 hours, or overnight.

23 Draw the tartan design on the hat and kilt using the red and black food colouring pens.

24 Using the black food colouring pen, draw the eyes and eyelashes. Draw the eyebrows with the brown food colouring pen.

25 Rub a little of the red dusting powder on to his bottom, his cheeks and the tip of his nose.

Alternative designs:

This wonderfully cheeky Scotsman would be hard to improve upon. However, the alternatives I would suggest are to remove his beard and just have a bolder and more striking moustache, one that really curls up at the ends! The colouring of his tartan could be altered to suit your taste — you can mix and match any of the food colouring pens you have to make a splendid design, yellow and blue on green fondant looks excellent.

Mud Wrestlers

Every man's dream? Let's hope they appreciate it if you make this cake for a stag night party.

You WILL NEED:
1 devil's food cake (size 1)
1.425kg (3lb 3oz) fondant icing
350g (12oz) modelling fondant
50g (2oz) royal icing
egg yellow, flesh, sky blue, brown and red food colouring paste
275g (10oz) butter cream
egg white or gum arabic
2 tablespoons clear alcohol, eg vodka or gin
275g (10oz) plain chocolate drops
red dusting powder
black, blue, yellow, green, brown and red food colouring pens

EQUIPMENT:
7–8 cocktail sticks
30 cm (12 inch) square cake board
ruler
No. 3 piping nozzle
fine paintbrush
medium paintbrush
No. 42 shell piping nozzle
4 12 cm (5 inch) wooden skewers or dowelling
gold embroidery thread

COLOUR:
Fondant icing: 1.425kg (3lb 3oz) cream (a touch of egg yellow)
Modelling fondant: 225g (8oz) flesh, 75g (3oz) white, 50g (2oz) sky blue
Royal icing: 25g (1oz) cream, 25g (1oz) reddish brown

1 Cover the cake board with 350g (12oz) of the cream fondant. Indent the lines for the wooden flooring with a ruler. Mark the joins and the wood grain with the end of a cocktail stick and the nails with the tip of the No. 3 piping nozzle. Leave to dry.

2 Slice the top off the cake so it is completely flat. Split and fill the cake with three-quarters of the butter cream, then spread a thin layer all over the cake to help the fondant stick and to seal the cake to prevent crumbs.

3 Roll out 275g (10oz) of the cream fondant. Place the top of the cake down on to it and cut round. Place the cake on the cake board, right side up. Roll out the trimmings thickly and cut out 2 sets of steps. Leave to dry.

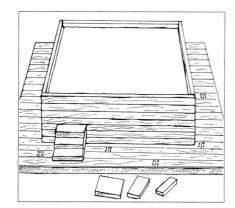

4 Roll out 200g (7oz) of the cream fondant. Measure the back of the cake and cut a piece to fit. Indent the lines for the wood with a ruler and mark the wood grain with the end of a cocktail stick. Lift carefully and place on the back of the cake, letting the top over-

lap slightly. Repeat for the sides, then the front. Stick the steps in place with a little egg white or gum arabic.

5 With the flesh-coloured modelling fondant, roll 2 sausage shapes using 75g (3oz) for each, and cut the legs about half way up. Cut the arms at the sides, then shape the bodies. Roll 2 balls using 15g (1/2oz) each for the heads. Model 4 boobs, 2 tiny noses and 4 nipples. Position the girls on the cake in their poses. With the end of a cock-tail stick, mark the belly buttons and a smile on the redhead's face. With the tip of the No. 3 piping nozzle, mark the blonde's mouth. Stick the heads, noses, boobs and nipples in place using a lit-tle egg white or gum arabic.

6 Put the clear alcohol into a bowl and mix with a little brown food colouring paste. Using the medium paintbrush, paint the sides of the ring, the cake board and the steps to look like wood.

7 With the cream royal icing and the No. 42 shell piping nozzle, pipe the blonde hair.

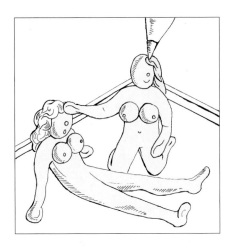

8 With the reddish brown royal icing and the No. 3 piping nozzle, pipe the redhead's hair.

9 Using two-thirds of the white modelling fondant, make 2 buckets with the top of each slightly hollow. Leave to dry. With the remaining fondant, cut out 5 posters and stick in place on the sides of the ring.

10 With the sky blue modelling fondant, model another bucket as before and cut out 2 towels. Fringe the ends by making small cuts and mark the lines with a knife. Fold into shape and put one in place on the board, setting the other aside.

11 Reserving 4 of the chocolate drops, melt the rest in a bowl over a saucepan of hot water. Allow to cool slightly, then spoon into the wrestling ring, swirling around and over the girls to look like mud. Fill the 3 buckets with

chocolate and stick in place, with some chocolate spilt on the floor.

12 Stick the 4 wooden skewers or dowelling into the corners of the wrestling ring. Tie the gold embroidery thread at the back and wind it round the 4 corners twisting twice round each skewer to secure. Repeat for the top rope.

13 Stick the reserved chocolate drops on top of the skewers with a little melted chocolate. Put the sky blue towel in place over the skewer at the back to hide the rope ties.

14 Leave the cake to dry for at least 8 hours, or overnight.

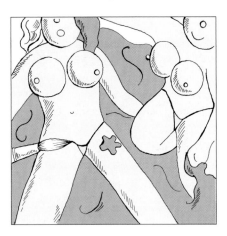

15 Mix a little of the sky blue food colouring paste with a few drops of clear alcohol. Using a fine paintbrush, paint the girls' modest bikini bottoms in place.

16 Dust the girls' cheeks and their top-heavy assets with a little red dusting powder.

17 Using the various food colouring pens, draw on the girls' eyes and eyebrows and the designs on the posters around the sides of the ring.

Alternative designs:

A naughty suggestion for this cake would be to replace the mud on these wickedly muddy wrestlers with green slime! Take some clear piping gel and colour it a light green. Replace the melted chocolate mud with the coloured gel and hey presto you have a cake with lady 'slime wrestlers' — what could be more fun! If you don't fancy being quite so adventurous, just change the colour of the bikinis and paint them a bright red or green.

Right: Mud wrestlers

Party Surprise

Not only will he get a big birthday cake, but a big girl to go with it, too, to tickle his fancy!

You will need:

2 rich fruit cakes or 2 Victoria sponge cakes (size1, size 2)

1.1kg (2lb 7oz) fondant icing

75g (3oz) modelling fondant

125g (4oz) royal icing

flesh and black food colouring paste

4 tablespoons apricot glaze (for the rich fruit cake and Victoria sponge cake)

1.025kg (2lb 4oz) marzipan (for the rich fruit cake)

275g (10oz) Continental butter cream (for the Victoria sponge cake)

2 tablespoons clear alcohol, eg vodka or gin (for the rich fruit cake)

egg white or gum arabic

black food colouring pen

pink dusting powder

Equipment:

2–3 cocktail sticks

30 cm (12 inch) round cake board

pastry brush

fine paintbrush

7 x 12 cm (3 x 5 inch) piece of bright pink voile net (tulle)

rice paper

greaseproof paper

scissors

No. 2 piping nozzle

17 pink ribbon bows

Colour:

Fondant icing: 1.1kg (2lb 7oz) white

Modelling fondant: 75g (3oz) flesh

Royal icing: 125g (4oz) black

1 Cover the cake board with 350g (12oz) of the white fondant and leave to dry.

2 Slice the tops off the cakes so they are completely flat.

3 If you have made rich fruit cakes, brush both cakes with the apricot glaze, then cover with marzipan (see page 18) and leave to dry for 24 hours. Place the larger cake in the centre of the cake board.

4 If you have made Victoria sponge cakes, split and fill the 2 cakes with the Continental butter cream. Place the larger of the two cakes in the centre of the cake board. Brush both cakes with the apricot glaze to help the fondant stick.

5 For the rich fruit cakes, brush the marzipan with clear alcohol to sterilize and help the fondant stick.

6 Roll out the white fondant and cover the bottom tier. Trim neatly round the bottom edge. Cover the smaller cake with the remaining white fondant and again neatly trim round the bottom edge. Place on top of the bottom tier.

7 To make the girl, cut off one-sixth of the modelling fondant and roll a ball for her head, model her boobs, nipples and a tiny nose. Mark her smile with a cocktail stick. Roll the remaining modelling fondant into a sausage shape. Make a cut half way down for the legs. Flatten the top slightly and cut away the arms from the sides. Model the body shape and place on the top of the cake in a kneeling position, with the legs to one side. Stick her head and nose, boobs and nipples in place with a little egg white or gum arabic.

8 Fold the piece of voile net in half lengthways and wrap round the girl, tucking the end under her hand.

9 Cut an 11 cm (4½ inch) diameter circle of rice paper and make tears in it from the centre outwards. Carefully place over the top of the girl and stick to the surface of the cake with a little egg white or gum arabic.

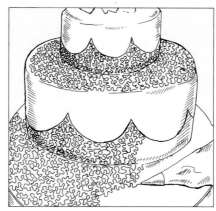

13 Pipe the girl's hair and pony tail with the remaining black royal icing. Leave the hair to dry thoroughly before adding the pink bow otherwise the ribbon will soak up the black colouring and stain.

14 Leave the cake to dry for at least 8 hours, or overnight to allow the icing to set firmly.

15 Carefully draw on the girl's eyes and eyebrows with the black food colouring pen. Gently dust a little of the pink dusting powder on to her cheeks and boobs.

16 Stick the ribbon bow in place in the girl's hair with a little egg white or gum arabic.

10 To decorate the sides, you need to make 2 templates from the greaseproof paper, see below. Cut a long strip about 5 cm (2 inches) deep, place round the bottom tier and cut to size. Repeat for the top tier. Fold each strip in half 3 times. Cut out a half circle from one end, curving up to the opposite corner. Unfold and position around each tier, securing with the tip of a pin. Take care not to let the pin go into the cake.

11 With the black royal icing and the No. 2 piping nozzle, pipe the loops around each tier following the grease-proof paper template. When all the loops are piped, carefully remove the template and pipe the cornelli work, see page 25 for clear instructions. Pipe a little on to the voile net.

12 Stick the bows in place round each tier with a little of the royal icing.

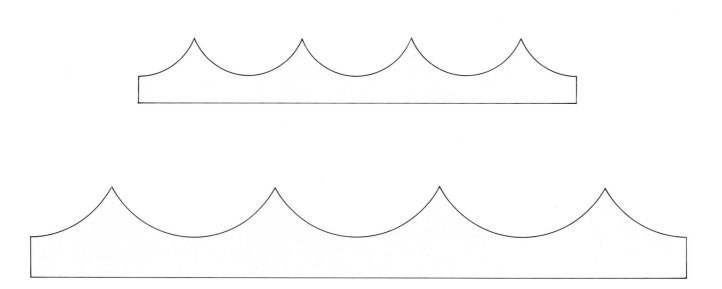

These templates show you half the length you will need for both the top and bottom tier. Use these guidelines and follow the instructions in step 10.

Roman Fantasy

Every fella would love to be pampered like this, but if you're anything like me, this cake will be as far as it goes!

You will need:

1 Madeira cake (size 4) or 1 quick mix cake (size 3)
1.025kg (2lb 4oz) fondant icing
240g (8½oz) modelling fondant
50g (2oz) royal icing
flesh, egg yellow, black and green food colouring paste
275g (10oz) butter cream
egg white or gum arabic
black food colouring pen
2 teaspoons clear alcohol, eg vodka or gin
gold and silver lustre powder

Equipment:

3–4 cocktail sticks
30 cm (12 inch) square cake board
fine and medium paintbrush
No. 3 piping nozzle
3 15 cm (6 inch) plaster cake pillars

Colour:

Fondant icing: 1.025kg (2lb 4oz) white
Modelling fondant: 200g (7oz) white, 40g (1½oz) flesh
Royal icing: 40g (1½oz) cream (a touch of egg yellow), 15g (½oz) black

1 Slice the top off the cake so it is completely flat.

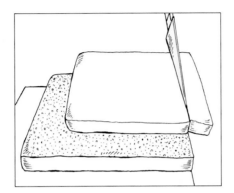

2 Slice a layer in the cake. Put the first layer on the cake board at one corner, allowing room for a layer of fondant icing on the side of the cake. Place the second layer on top, pushed back to form a 5 cm (2 inch) step. Trim the cake at the back to match the first layer.

3 Spread half of the butter cream in the layer, then spread a thin layer all over the cake to help the fondant stick.

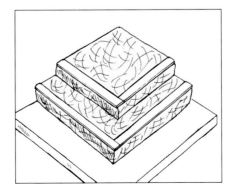

4 Roll out 125g (4oz) of the white fondant icing about 3 mm (⅛ inch) thick and cut 2 strips, 1.5 cm (¾ inch) wide, for the raised steps on each layer. Place on the cake, letting the edges overlap, as shown.

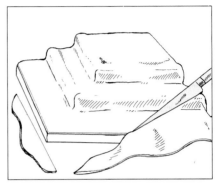

5 Roll out the remaining white fondant and cover the cake and board completely, smoothing round the steps with your hands. Trim round the edge of the board and leave to dry.

6 Meanwhile, to make the bed, use 125g (4oz) of the white modelling fondant to model an oblong shape about 5 x 8 cm (2 x 3½ inches) and 2 cm (¾ inch) deep. Mark the lines all round with a knife, then place on the cake.

7 Model the 3 gowns using 20g (¾oz) for each. Pinch a little up on one side for the shoulder tie.

8 With the remaining white modelling fondant, model a tiny cone shape for the base of the grapes and set aside, then roll out and cut a heart-shaped fan and an oblong for the pillow. Indent a line down the middle of the fan, using a cocktail stick. Roll up the pillow and press in the centre where the head will rest. Stick the pillow and white gowns in position with egg white or gum arabic.

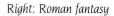

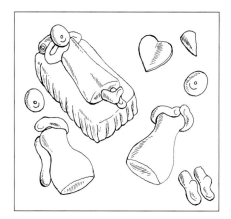

his laurel wreath and edge the top of his gown. Paint the fan and loops at the base of the bed.

9 With the flesh-coloured modelling fondant, roll 3 balls for the heads, using 5g (¹/₄ oz) for each. Mark the smiles with a cocktail stick. Roll 3 tiny noses. Model the man's feet and stick in position, one on top of the other. Model 2 tiny feet for the kneeling handmaiden. Roll 6 sausage shapes and model the shoulders and arms, making 2 slightly longer for the handmaidens' chests. Stick everything in place using a little egg white or gum arabic, including the fan and cone shape made earlier.

10 With the cream royal icing and the No. 3 piping nozzle, pipe the hair for the man and one handmaiden. Pipe dots on the cone for the grapes. Reserve a little of the royal icing for positioning the pillars.

11 With the black royal icing and the No. 3 piping nozzle, pipe the hair for the kneeling handmaiden, letting it spiral down her back.

12 Leave the cake to dry for at least 8 hours, or overnight.

13 With the black food colouring pen, draw the eyes and eyebrows on the three figures.

14 Mix the silver and gold lustre powders with a teaspoon each of the clear alcohol. Using a fine paintbrush, paint the marbled pattern effect all over the surface of the cake. Carefully paint a little gold on to the man's head for

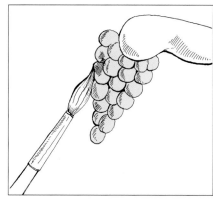

15 Mix a tiny amount of the green food colouring paste with a few drops of water or clear alcohol to make an even colour and use to paint the grapes with a fine paintbrush.

16 Dust the whole of the cake with the dry gold lustre powder using a medium-sized paintbrush, and applying a little more powder along the painted marbled lines.

17 Position the three pillars on the cake as illustrated in the main pictures, and secure them firmly with a dab of the reserved royal icing.

Alternative design:

You could add detail to the pillars by painting the marbled design over them. Or, as pictured, pipe a wreath around each of them. Use 25g (1oz) of green royal icing to decorate 3-4 pillars. First, pipe a built-up circle using a No. 2 piping nozzle, then using a greaseproof piping bag with a small 'v' trimmed from the tip, pipe the leaves.

Give us a Kiss

How about blowing a kiss to your favourite fella with this fabulous pair of pouting lips!

YOU WILL NEED:
1 Madeira cake (size 9)
750g (1lb 11oz) fondant icing
50g (2oz) modelling fondant
red and black food colouring paste
150g (5oz) butter cream
egg white or gum arabic

EQUIPMENT:
2 cocktail sticks
25 cm (10 inch) round cake board
fine paintbrush

COLOUR:
Fondant icing: 250g (9oz) white,
   500g (1lb 2oz) red
Modelling fondant: 40g (1½oz) black,
   10g (½oz) red

1 Cover the cake board with the white fondant and leave to dry.

2 Slice the top off the cake so it is completely flat.

3 Cut 4 corners off the cake, each strip measuring 10 cm (4 inches).

4 Cut a small diamond shape out of the centre of the cake, then cut a slight 'V' from the top lip to give it shape.

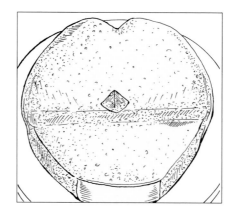

5 In the middle, cut a dip the width of the cake about 1 cm (½ inch) deep to separate the 2 lips. Trim the edge of the cake to round off.

6 Spread the butter cream all over the cake to help the fondant stick and to seal the cake to prevent crumbs.

7 To pad out the lips, model a heart shape with 25g (1oz) of the red fondant icing and press on to the centre of the top lip. Taking 2 more 25g (1oz) heart-shaped pieces, press one on each side of the bottom lip. Cut another 25g (1oz) heart-shaped piece in half and

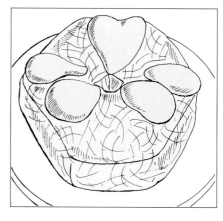

press on either side of the top lip, as shown in the diagram above.

8 Roll out the remaining red fondant icing, lift carefully and cover the entire cake, smoothing with your hands, then trim. Place the cake in the centre of the cake board.

9 Using the end of the paintbrush, mark the lines for the 'pucker' creases.

10 To make the lipstick base, take 25g (1oz) of the black modelling fondant, roll into a sausage shape and trim the ends straight with a sharp knife. Indent a line at the top with a knife. Roll the remaining black fondant into a slightly thinner sausage shape and again trim the ends straight.

11 With the red modelling fondant, model the top of the lipstick. Stick the pieces together using a little egg white or gum arabic.

12 Leave the cake to dry for at least 8 hours, or overnight.

Nudist Beach

This saucy seaside cake is sure to raise a sunny smile on even the dullest of winter days.

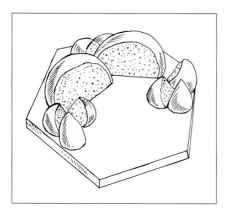

You will need:

3 Madeira cakes (size 6, size 8)
725g (1lb 10oz) fondant icing
350g (12oz) modelling fondant
150g (5oz) royal icing
black, yellow, red, flesh, blue, brown and egg yellow food colouring paste
375g (13oz) butter cream
125g (4oz) soft light brown sugar
egg white or gum arabic
gold lustre powder
black and red food colouring pens
2 tablespoons clear piping jelly

Equipment:

9–10 cocktail sticks
30 cm (12 inch) hexagonal cake board
7 cm (3 inch) plain circle cutter
washing liquid ball dispenser or smooth tennis ball
fine and medium paintbrush
7 cm (3 inch) skewer or dowelling pastry brush
No. 3 piping nozzle
No. 42 shell piping nozzle

Colour:

Fondant icing: 725g (1lb 10oz) grey (a touch of black)
Modelling fondant: 75g (3oz) yellow, 50g (2oz) red, 150g (5oz) flesh, 25g (1oz) blue, 5g (¼oz) black, 20g (¾oz) white
Royal icing: 25g (1oz) brown, 25g (1oz) cream (a touch of egg yellow), 50g (2oz) pale blue, 25g (1oz) white
Clear piping jelly: 2 tablespoons blue

1 Slice the tops off the cakes so they are completely flat.

2 Cut the large bowl cake exactly in half and place on the cake board at an angle near the back. Cut the 2 small bowl cakes into quarters and arrange the pieces on the cake board as shown in the illustration.

3 Using three-quarters of the butter cream, spread a layer over the surface of the cakes to help the fondant stick.

4 Roll out the grey fondant and cover the cakes completely, smoothing down into the crevices with your fingers. Pinch the icing to form rock shapes.

5 Spread the remaining butter cream over the sand area and a little on to the rocks to allow the brown sugar sand

to stick. Carefully sprinkle the brown sugar all over, building it up slightly deeper near the rocks. Press down with the back of a spoon. Leave an uncovered strip at the front of the board for the sea.

6 To make the parasol, roll out half of the yellow modelling fondant and cut out a circle using the 7 cm (3 inch) circle cutter. Place the circle on to the ball and press all round the edge to scallop the parasol. Carefully indent the lines with a knife and set aside to dry. With the trimmings, roll a ball about the size of a marble. Paint a little egg white or gum arabic on to the end of the 7 cm (3 inch) skewer or dowelling and push it gently into the ball of fondant. Leave to dry with the parasol.

7 With the remaining yellow modelling fondant, cut out a beach towel, marking the lines at each end with a knife, and position on the sand. Model a pair of boxer shorts. Roll a ball with 15g (½ oz) and cut into quarters for the beach balls.

8 Roll a 15g (½oz) ball of the red modelling fondant, and cut into quarters. Stick alternate red and yellow quarters together with egg white or gum arabic to make the 2 beach balls.

9 With the remaining red modelling fondant, cut another beach towel and make small even cuts at either end to fringe. Indent the lines with a knife and place on the board.

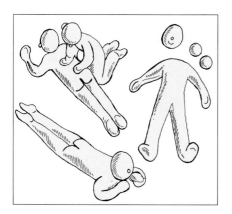

10 Each body, excluding the head (and extras!), is made with 25g (1oz) of the flesh-coloured modelling fondant. Roll into a sausage shape and make a cut half way down for the legs. Flatten the top slightly and cut away the arms from the sides. Model the body shapes and bend into their poses. Divide the remaining 25g (1oz) into 5 pieces. Roll 4 pieces into balls for the heads and mark the smiles with a cocktail stick. With the one remaining piece of fondant, model all the noses and 2 boobs. Stick everything in place with a little egg white or gum arabic.

11 Make a towel and a small book with the blue modelling fondant. Position the towel on the rocks and place the book on the topless woman's lap. Put the yellow boxer shorts on the blue towel.

12 With the black modelling fondant, model the binoculars, the sunglasses, a pair of knickers and the suntan lotion bottle. Stick everything in place with a little egg white or gum arabic.

13 With the white modelling fondant, make 2 sunhats, a folded newspaper and 5 tiny shells. Mark the patterns on the shells with a cocktail stick. Stick everything in place.

14 To give a sparkle as if the sun were shining, brush a little of the gold lustre powder over the sand and shells, using the pastry brush.

15 With the brown royal icing and the No. 3 piping nozzle, pipe the hair on the two men.

16 With the cream royal icing and the No. 42 shell piping nozzle, pipe the women's hair.

17 Lift the parasol off the ball on which it was drying and stick the parasol base to the underside with a little royal icing. Leave to dry upside down.

18 Using a round-bladed knife, spread the pale blue royal icing on the edge of the board for the sea, flicking it up slightly near the rocks. Mark the wavy lines with a cocktail stick.

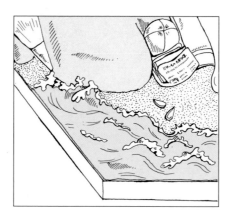

19 With the white royal icing and the No. 3 piping nozzle, pipe the froth on the sea, following the ripples.

20 Leave the cake to dry for at least 8 hours, or overnight.

21 With the black pen, draw the eyes and eyebrows, the writing on the newspaper and on the book cover.

22 With the red food colouring pen, draw the stripes on the boxer shorts, the dots on the boobs and underline the newspaper heading. Draw the flower pattern on the parasol and push the end of the skewer into the cake directly behind the topless woman.

23 Using a medium paintbrush, paint the blue piping jelly over the blue sea, building up the thickness in some parts to make it look deeper. Leave to set.

Communal Shower

You'd have to be double-jointed to join in this shower party, but come clean — you know you'd enjoy it!

You will need:

1 Madeira cake (size 4)
1.4kg (3lb 2oz) fondant icing
675g (1lb 8oz) modelling fondant
50g (2oz) royal icing
black, blue, green, brown, yellow, red, mauve and flesh food colouring paste
450g (1lb) butter cream
1 tablespoon clear alcohol, eg vodka or gin
egg white or gum arabic
black food colouring pen

Equipment:

9-10 cocktail sticks
25 cm (10 inch) square cake board
ruler
small piece of foam
crimping tool
fine paintbrush
No. 3 piping nozzle
daisy cutter

Colour:

Fondant icing: 1.32kg (2lb 15oz) white, 75g (3oz) grey
Modelling fondant: 50g (2oz) brown, 100g (3½oz) yellow, 65g (2½oz) turquoise (equal quantities of blue and green), 275g (10oz) white, 25g (1oz) red, 40g (1½oz) mauve, 25g (1oz) black, 75g (3oz) flesh
Royal icing: 50g (2oz) white

1 Cover the cake board with 275g (10oz) of the white fondant icing. Mark the lines for the tiles with a long ruler. Leave to dry.

2 Slice the top off the cake so it is completely flat.

3 Cut the cake exactly in half, then trim 4 cm (1½ inches) from the length of each cake.

4 Sandwich the cakes together with 225g (8oz) of the butter cream. Stand the cake upright and check it stands straight. If it doesn't, trim the bottom to make it even. Spread a thin layer of butter cream over the surface of the cake to help the fondant stick and to seal the cake to prevent crumbs.

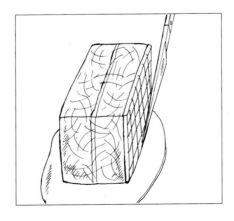

5 Roll out 250g (9oz) of the white fondant icing and mark the lines for the tiles with a long ruler. Cut a straight line at the bottom and along one side, turn the icing over, then place the back of the shower cake down on to the icing, lining up the straight edges. Carefully trim to fit.

6 Cover the 2 sides, and then the front of the shower in the same way. You may find it helpful to move the cake using 2 cake smoothers, so that your hands don't mark the patterned icing. Carefully cut out the shower door from the front of the cake, leaving 2 tiles all round the edge.

7 Place the cake in position on the cake board. Roll out the remaining white fondant icing with the trimmings. Measure the top of the cake, and carefully cut out a piece of fondant to fit. Mark the tiles as before, then place on the cake, lining up the tiles.

8 Measure the shower door opening and cover it with the rolled out grey fondant icing.

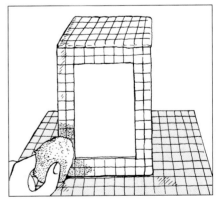

9 Mix a little of both the blue and green food colouring paste with the clear alcohol. Dip the small piece of foam into the colour, squeeze out the excess, then gently wipe the foam evenly over the tiles, taking care to keep the colour out of the marked lines. Allow to dry thoroughly.

10 To make the basket, roll the brown modelling fondant into a ball and hollow out the top slightly by pushing gently with your thumb. Using the crimping tool, crimp round the outside, letting the tool spring open to create the lines. Crimp a line around the top, then position the basket on the cake board.

11 Roll out the yellow modelling fondant and cut out 3 oblong shapes for the towels. Fold 2 in half, then roll them up, placing one on the cake board and the other in the basket. Mark lines on the remaining towel with a cocktail stick and arrange in a crumpled heap on the board.

12 Roll out the turquoise modelling fondant and cut out 2 more towels. Fold and roll as before and stick one in the basket and the other beside it.

13 Roll out 15g (¹/₂ oz) of the white modelling fondant and cut a strip about 7 cm (3 inches) long. Stick to the side of the shower using a little egg white or gum arabic. Model 3 hooks with the trimmings, and stick in place. Divide another 15g (¹/₂ oz) piece into 4 and model the socks, then stick in place. Roll a thin sausage shape with a further 15g (¹/₂ oz) and stick above the shower door for the curtain pole. Roll out 40g (1¹/₂ oz) and cut out a triangular shape. Drape over the middle hook on the side of the shower and stick firmly in place.

14 Roll out the red modelling fondant and cut out a pair of boxer shorts and a basque. Mark the criss-cross pattern on the basque with a knife. Model the 2 straps. Stick everything in place with a little egg white or gum arabic.

15 Roll out the mauve modelling fondant, cut a triangular shape, stick in place, draped over the end hook.

16 Using the black modelling fondant, model 2 bra cups, 2 pairs of knickers and a pair of boxer shorts. Stick in place with a little egg white or gum arabic.

17 Divide the flesh-coloured modelling fondant into 8 equal pieces. Model 5 arms and 3 legs. Using the white royal icing and the No. 3 piping nozzle, stick all the limbs in position, as shown above.

18 For the shower curtain, roll out the remaining white modelling fondant and cut an oblong measuring 15 x 18 cm (6 x 7 inches). Press the daisy cutter gently into the fondant to make the pattern. Pinch the top to pleat. Stick the shower curtain in place with royal icing. With the No. 3 piping nozzle and the white royal icing pipe the shower rings at the top. Leave the cake to dry for at least 8 hours, or overnight.

19 With the black food colouring pen, draw the bra straps and the stripes on the red boxer shorts.

Alternative design:

This cake would be fun to give to somebody at the end of the football season — just alter it to represent the changing rooms at the end of a match! Crumple up the towels into messy piles, make pairs of shorts and football shirts (in the appropriate colours) and lay them higgledy-piggledy — finally dust everything with cocoa powder to make things look as dirty as possible!

Right: Communal shower

Whose Turn on Top?

At any angle, this cake looks interesting — whether you're promising a night to remember, or just like having your toes nibbled!

You will need:
1 quick mix cake (size 4)
1.6kg (3lb 9oz) fondant icing
black, flesh, egg yellow, orange and
   brown food colouring paste
200g (7 oz) butter cream
egg white or gum arabic

Equipment:
6-7 cocktail sticks
35 cm (14 inch) round cake board

scissors
greaseproof paper
fine paintbrush

Colour:
Fondant icing: 375g (13oz) black,
   1kg (2lb 4oz) flesh,
   225g (8oz) cream (a touch of egg
   yellow)

1 Cover the cake board with the black fondant icing. Put to one side and leave to dry thoroughly.

2 Carefully slice the top off the cake where it has risen so that it is completely flat, then slice the cake in half to make 2 layers.

3 Draw the feet outline on to a large piece of greaseproof paper and then carefully cut out the shapes. The feet should be approximately 20 cm (8 inches) long.

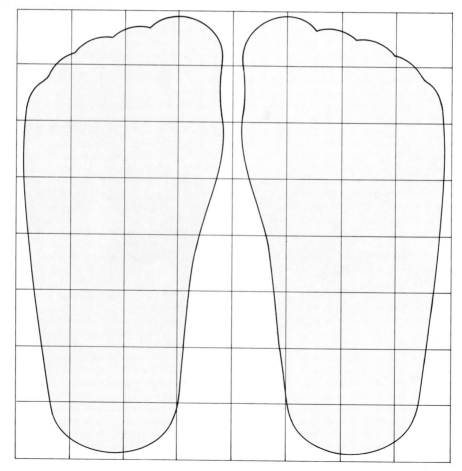

I square
= 2.5cm (1 inch)

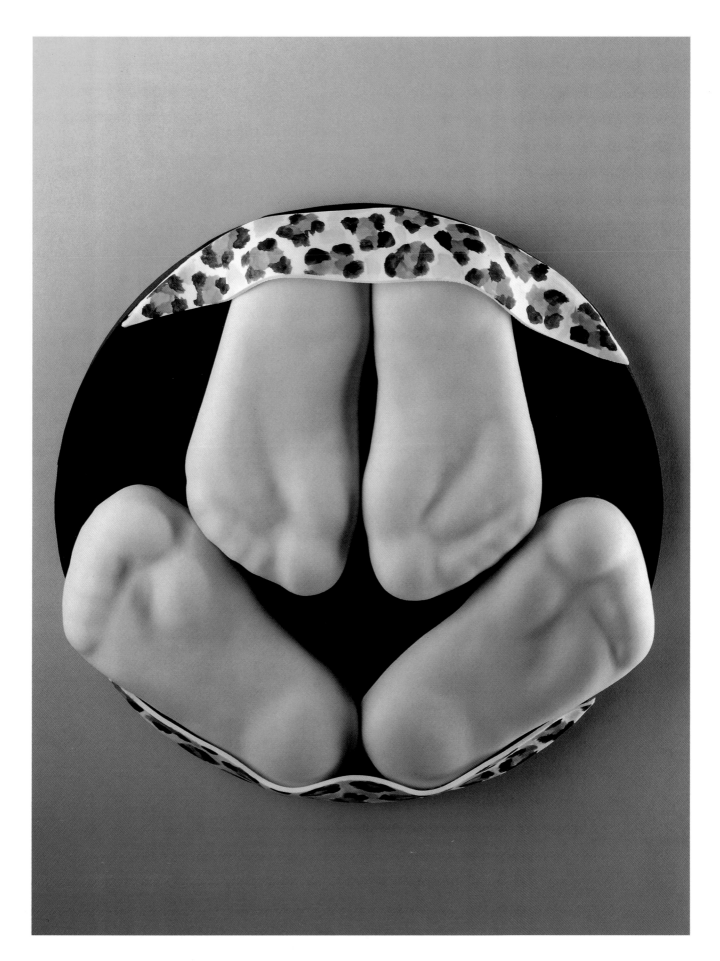

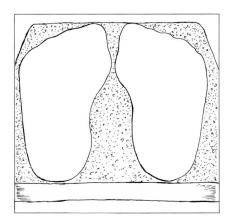

4 Place the templates of both feet on to one of the cakes, as shown above, and cut out. Then place the templates on to the other cake and cut out 2 more feet.

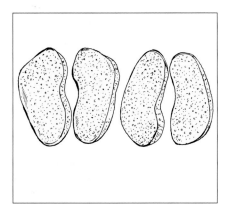

5 Trim each cake slightly to round off the edges, then cut a gentle dip for the arch of the foot in all 4 feet.

6 Spread butter cream thinly all over the cakes to help the fondant stick.

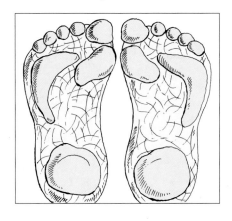

7 Pad out each foot with 50g (2oz) of the flesh-coloured fondant. Divide the

50g (2oz) piece into 5. Roll 1 piece into a ball for the heel and flatten slightly. Press on to the bottom of the foot and smooth the edges. Model 2 pieces for above the arch and press on to the cake, smoothing the edges. Roll another piece into a ball and place on the cake for the big toe. Split the remaining piece into 4 and place on the cake for the smaller toes, as shown above. Repeat for the other 3 feet.

8 Roll out 200g (7oz) of the flesh-coloured fondant and cover a foot, smoothing the shape with your hands. Repeat for the other 3 feet. Place each foot in position on the cake board.

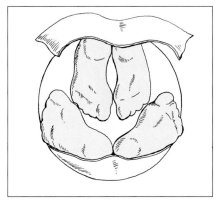

9 Roll out the cream-coloured fondant into a strip about 30 cm (12 inches) long and 20 cm (8 inches) wide and cut in half lengthways. With the straight edges facing inwards, drape the strips of fondant just over the feet to look like the edges of sheets and stick in place using a little egg white or gum arabic. Trim to neaten the edges if necessary.

10 Leave the cake to dry for at least 8 hours, or overnight to allow the icing to set firmly.

11 Blend a little of each of the orange, brown and black food colouring pastes with a few drops of water. Use these to paint the leopard print pattern on to the sheets using a fine paintbrush. Leave to dry.

Alternative designs:

The jazzy sheets for this rather naughty cake can be changed to make them marginally less wicked. Paint them instead with a pretty floral design, or simple, multi-coloured dots. You can use your own choice of colours but pink and green is always a good combination. However, if you want to remain in the raunchy mode, why not paint them black with little red hearts or red with little white hearts — the variations are endless!

Bedtime Woes

Even if long lie-ins are a thing of the past, anybody with small children will have a good giggle over this cake!

You will need:

1 Madeira cake (size 3) or 1 quick mix cake (size 2)
1.275kg (2lb 13oz) fondant icing
200g (7oz) modelling fondant
75g (3oz) royal icing
125g (4oz) pastillage icing
mauve, flesh, egg yellow, brown and pink food colouring paste
200g (7oz) butter cream
egg white or gum arabic
mauve and black food colouring pens
pink dusting powder

Equipment:

5-6 cocktail sticks
18 cm (7 inch) and 15 cm (6 inch) greaseproof paper circles
small and medium heart cutters
foam sheet
25 x 35 cm (10 x 14 inch) oblong cake board
crimping tool
6 cm (2$^{1}/_{2}$ inch) plain circle cutter
fine paintbrush
blossom plunger cutter
5 white stamens
No. 3 piping nozzle

Colour:

Pastillage icing: 125g (4oz) white
Fondant icing: 350g (12oz) mauve, 925g (2lb 1oz) white
Modelling fondant: 25g (1oz) light mauve, 65g (2$^{1}/_{2}$oz) flesh, 5g ($^{1}/_{4}$oz) yellow, 15g ($^{1}/_{2}$oz) brown, 50g (2oz) pink, 15g ($^{1}/_{2}$oz) white
Royal icing: 25g (1oz) cream (a touch of egg yellow), 25g (1oz) brown, 25g (1oz) white

1 Roll out the pastillage icing and cut out a half circle using the 18 cm (7 inch) greaseproof paper circle as a template. Working quickly as this icing dries fast, cut out the headboard pattern with the heart cutters. Place on the foam sheet and let dry for at least 8 hours.

2 Cover the cake board with mauve fondant icing, reserve the trimmings. With a sharp knife, make small cuts round the edge for the carpet frill. Crimp a line following the frill. Leave to dry.

3 Slice the top off the cake so it is completely flat.

4 Measure 16 cm (6$^{1}/_{2}$inches) from one end of the cake and cut across the width, so you have a piece measuring 16 x 20 cm (6$^{1}/_{2}$ x 8 inches), and a

smaller piece. Taking the smaller cake, cut 2 circles using the 6 cm (2$^{1}/_{2}$ inch) circle cutter. Then cut 2 pillows measuring 6 x 4 cm (2$^{1}/_{2}$ x 1$^{1}/_{2}$ inches) and cut a slight dip for the head in each one. Then cut out 3 thin oblong shapes, 2 measuring 12 x 4 cm (5 x 1$^{1}/_{2}$ inches) and 1 measuring 5 x 4 cm (2 x 1$^{1}/_{2}$ inches), for the bodies. Place the bodies in position on the bed, sticking with a little butter cream.

5 Spread a thin layer of butter cream all over the cakes to help the fondant stick and prevent crumbs.

6 To make the sheet, roll out 225g (8oz) of the white fondant and cover the top part of the bed. Place the cake in the centre of the cake board.

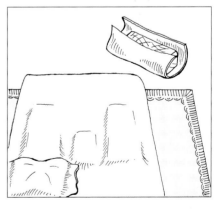

7 Roll out 175g (6oz) of the white fondant and cut in half. Place a pillow cake in the centre of each piece of fondant and fold the icing round the pillow. Trim the ends straight, sticking together with a little egg white or gum arabic. Place on the bed and mark the creases with a knife.

8 Place one of the round cakes on either side of the bed. To make the tablecloths, roll out 250g (9oz) of the white fondant and cut 2 circles using the 15 cm (6 inch) greaseproof paper circle as a template. Place a circle over the top of each round cake, encouraging the pleats.

9 With the white fondant trimmings, model the pages for the centre of the book and set aside to dry.

10 For the little girl, roll a ball with just over half of the light mauve modelling fondant and model the top of her body. With a 5g ($\frac{1}{4}$ oz) piece, model the 2 sleeves and mark the pleats with a cocktail stick. Stick in place on the bed with a little egg white or gum arabic.

11 Roll out the light mauve fondant trimmings and cut a cover for the book. Wrap round the pages made in step 9 and place on the table. Roll 2 tiny pompoms for the slippers and set aside.

12 For the little girl's neck, roll a tiny ball with some of the flesh-coloured modelling fondant and stick on to the top of her nightgown .

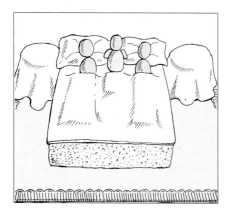

13 Divide a 50g (2oz) piece of the flesh-coloured fondant into 5 and roll into balls. Use 2 for the tops of the adult bodies, pressing them down on to the bed to flatten slightly. Stick the remaining 3 in place for the heads, using a little egg white or gum arabic. Mark the mouths with a cocktail stick.

14 With the remaining flesh-coloured fondant, roll 3 tiny balls for the noses and model the arm for each adult and the little girl's hands. Set the girl's hands to one side, and stick everything else in place with a little egg white or gum arabic.

15 To make the bed cover, roll out the remaining white fondant and cut out an oblong measuring 20 x 28 cm (8 x 11 inches). Trim the corners to round off. Lift gently and place over the bed, encouraging some pleats. Tuck round the bodies and stick the little girl's hands in place, pressing down gently on the cover.

16 With the yellow modelling fondant, make the teddy bear. Indent the ears with the end of a paintbrush.

17 With the brown modelling fondant, model the little girl's hair, marking a criss-cross pattern down each plait with a knife. Stick on to her head using a little egg white or gum arabic. Stick the teddy in place.

18 With the pink modelling fondant, roll 2 15g ($\frac{1}{2}$ oz) balls for the lampbases. Model a vase and push a cocktail stick into the centre to make room for the flowers. Model 2 tiny bows for the little girl's hair. Model the slippers and stick on the pompoms made in step 11. Stick everything in place on the cake board using a little egg white or gum arabic.

19 Model a cup and saucer with the white modelling fondant and set aside to dry. Roll out and cut 5 flowers with the blossom plunger cutter. Push a stamen through the centre of each and secure with a little egg white or gum arabic. Leave to dry upside down.

20 With the mauve fondant trimmings, model the 2 lampshades. Mark the pleats all round with a cocktail stick and set aside to dry.

21 With the cream-coloured royal icing and the No. 3 piping nozzle, pipe the woman's hair.

22 With the brown royal icing and the No. 3 piping nozzle, pipe the man's hair. Leave the cake to dry for at least 8 hours, or overnight.

23 With the white royal icing and the No. 3 piping nozzle, stick the headboard, cup and saucer and the lampshades in place. Arrange the flowers in the vase.

24 Mix the pink food colouring paste with a few drops of water and, using a fine paintbrush, paint all the roses on the bedcover.

25 Draw the bedcover trim, bows and dots with the mauve food colouring pen. Draw the eyes and eyebrows with the black food colouring pen. Brush a little pink dusting powder on to the figures' cheeks.

Right: Bedtime woes

Useful Suppliers and Addresses

Blue Ribbons Cakecraft Centre
110 Walton Road
East Molesey KT8 0HP
Tel: 081 941 1591

Blackburn's Cake Centre
108 Alexandra Drive
Surbiton KT5 9AG
Tel: 081 399 6875

Mary Jane's Pantry
60 Church Road
Ashford
Middlesex TW15 2TS
Tel: 0784 252904

Squires Kitchen
3 Waverley Lane
Farnham
Surrey GU9 8BB
Tel: 0252 734309

Felicity Clare
360 Leach Place
Walton Summit, Bamber Bridge
Preston
Lancashire PR5 8AR
Tel: 0772 628286

A Piece of Cake
18 Upper High Street
Thame
Oxfordshire
OX9 3EX
Tel: 0844 213428

Elizabeth David Cookshop
3 North Row
The Market
Covent Garden
London WC2 8RA
Tel: 071 836 9167

G. T. Culpitt & Son Ltd.
Culpitt House
Place Farm
Wheathamstead
Hertfordshire
AL4 8SB
Tel: 0582 834122

British Sugarcraft Guild
Wellington House
Messeter Place
Eltham
London
SE9 5DP
Tel: 081 859 6943

North America
Maid of Scandinavia
3244 Raleigh Avenue
Minneapolis
MN 55416

Wilton Enterprises Inc
2240 West 75th Street
Woodridge
Illinois 60517

Home Cake Artistry Inc
1002 North Central
Suite 511
Richardson
Texas 75080

Creative Tools Ltd.
3 Tannery Court
Richmond Hill
Ontario
Canada L4C 7V5

Australia
Australian National Cake Decorators'
Association
PO Box 321
Plympton SA5038

New Zealand
New Zealand Cake Decorators' Guild
Secretary Julie Tibble
78 Kirk Street
Otaki
Wellington

South Africa
South African Sugarcraft Guild
National Office
1 Tuzla Mews
187 Smit Street
Fairlan 2195

$\mathcal{I}ndex$

ACKNOWLEDGEMENTS
The Publisher would like to thank the following individuals and organizations for providing
the photographs used in this book:
Anthony Blake Photo Library /Graham Tann 25 left and right;
Food in Focus 7, 16 bottom left and right; Reed International Books Ltd.
/Paul Bussell 9, 22 top and bottom, 23, /Hilary Moore 21, /Peter Myers 15, 17 top right,
/Clive Streeter 11, 13, 17 top left, 19; Woman's Weekly 18, 24.